WHEN GOD CALLS YOU

WHEN GOD CALLS YOU FROM YOUR COMFORT ZONE

CARL HAYS

CITI OF BOOKS

CITIOFBOOKS, INC.
3736 Eubank NE Suite A1
Albuquerque, NM 87111-3579
www.citiofbooks.com
Hotline: 1 (877) 389-2759
Fax: 1 (505) 930-7244

Ordering Information:
Quantity sales. Special discounts are available on quantity purchases by corporations, associations, and others. For details, contact the publisher at the address above.

Printed in the United States of America.

ISBN-13:	Softcover	979-8-89391-635-5
	eBook	979-8-89391-636-2

Library of Congress Control Number: 2025907526

Table of Contents

About the Author

Carl Hays was born and grew up in a small rural town in Mendenhall, Mississippi. He received his formal education during the 1960s. Those were some of the most difficult and turbulent years in American history, probably only the second to slavery. It was a difficult time especially if you were a poor African American. It was known as the civil rights era.

In addition to the atrocious economic hardships in Mississippi, African Americans had to also deal with political and social discrimination issues. Blacks had no legal rights or access to adequate medical care. They were denied the most basic human rights afforded to other Americans. This was the America Carl Hays was born in and grew up in and would influence his future destiny.

Carl's father prayed weekly for his family and prayed that one of his six sons would become an attorney to deal with the unjust legal system. He also prayed that one of his six sons would become a doctor to deal with the insufficient and inadequate medical care for African Americans in Mississippi.

Carl's father knew the odds at that time of a young African American not having any money, and an inferior, substandard education was very unlikely to be accepted into law school and become an attorney. It was probably ten thousand to one. Carl's father influenced and prayed that his family would not consider the ten thousand but only consider the one, because he said, "You are the one." He would often say, "What appears to be impossible for man is never impossible for God."

Carl Hays did become "the one," that attorney, and another brother, Gregory, became that doctor. Both have been my father's answered prayer. They have also been awarded international patents for inventions to make life better for all mankind. Carl has written a number of articles and poems including "Our Story," "America, America Please Hear My Cry," "Johnny Took a Walk," "The Tragedy of Black America," "Falling from the Mountain Top," "If It Is Going to Be, It Is Up to Me," "We Made Plans," "Looking Out My window," "To Be a Friend," "Should African Americans Stand for the National Anthem," and "When Death Comes Calling."

I
Dedication

I dedicate this book, first to my family, my darling and faithful wife, Rhonda, whom I have had the joy and privilege of spending most of my life with. I know our lives together have not always been a bed of roses, but when I could not afford roses, you appreciatively, graciously, and humbly accepted tulips. We faced many hills, but each time I climbed a hill, I was able to overcome because you were right there by my side, helping and encouraging me every step of the way. We had some tears to shed, but you were always there with a shoulder for me to cry on when I needed one. We had some dark days, but even on the darkest day, I had sunshine because I knew you were close by. We had some sad times, but you always reminded me that troubles only last a night and joy comes in the morning. My greatest joy over the years has been each morning when I awake I can turn over and see your face next to me. We've had some good times, and those moments I will cherish forever.

Lionel Richie may have said you are "three times a lady," but you have been much more than three times a lady to me. Larry Graham may have said "you are one in a million," but you are much more than that for me. Eddie Kendricks came a little closer in describing you by saying, "You are my everything." Rhonda, you have been my everything, but much more than that, Rhonda, you have been the reason for my living, the wind beneath my wings.

Rhonda, thank you for being my love, my wife, and my friend. But most of all, thank you for allowing me to do it my way and for allowing me to be me.

Thank you,

Rhonda.

I love you and I dedicate this book to you.

To My Three Darling Angels, Carlameta, Sabrina, and Alana

Since children don't come with a set of instructions, I would like to thank my three daughters for allowing me to learn how to be a parent by practicing on them. However children really do come with a set of instructions; it is referred to as the Bible.

In the book, I explain how much of what my father learned about being a parent came from what he observed from his parents. His father was the son of a former slave. Slaves were taught very few parenting skills; therefore, my dad made a lot of mistakes as a parent because he had no role model to follow. But after considering all he had to overcome, I think he made a pretty good father. So I would be remiss if I did not also dedicate this book to my father.

I learned from my father and tried not to make the same mistakes I thought he made, but I am sure I made my share of parenting mistakes too. I pray that my girls learned from my mistakes and can be much better parents than I was.

To Carlameta

My first. Being the first, you faced the most difficult challenges, I am sure. Thank you for allowing me to be your father, and I hope once you read this book, you may understand that all parents make mistakes, but hopefully and prayerfully, you will be a better parent because of your experiences. I know we didn't always agree and still don't agree on all issues, but that is what makes us individuals and unique. The important thing to remember is the love and respect we have for each other are far more important than any issue of disagreement. I love you and you will always be my little angel.

Thank you,

Carlameta!

I love you and I dedicate this book to you.

To Sabrina

My second. I know you have always thought you were second-best, and your mother and I have tried to understand this from your perception. It is true, we brought you home and you had to share a room with your older sister. You had to sometimes wear your older sister's hand-me-down clothes and play with your older sister's toys. It may be true you had to wear your sister's clothes, play with her toys, and share a room, but the joy you brought into our lives opened a room in your mother's and father's hearts that you will never have to share with anyone. Thank you for being the joy of my life. You will always have your own private room in our hearts that we will not allow anyone to share.

One of my greatest treasures of life is the video you made titled "One Last Dance With My Dad." I will always keep and treasure that video.

Thank you,

Sabrina!

I love you and I dedicate this book to you.

Finally, to Alana

My last! Thank you for trying to be the peacemaker in the family. You have always accepted your mother and father's parenting mistakes and have tried to get your sisters to understand. Thank you for being yourself and allowing your parents to disagree with you without being disagreeable. Thank you for accepting your parents for what they are and not trying to change them to who you are. Baby boomers and millennials are very different. They think differently and act differently. Thank you for trying to teach us and get us to understand that. Thank you for understanding and accepting your parents for what we are. Although we don't always understand your thinking or agree with you, you are and always will be our loving bundle of joy.

Thank you,

Alana!

I love you and I dedicate this book to you.

To Evelyn,
My Sister / My Second Mom

In the Hays family, being the oldest girl meant you had to take on a lot of older-sister family responsibilities. Being the oldest girl meant you had to also serve as a second mom to all your younger brothers and sister. Being second mom meant you had to cook, wash, iron, clean house, and many other responsibilities.

My sister Evelyn graciously accepted and performed all these duties of an older sister, and I never once heard her complain. In addition to the house duties, she also took care of her younger brothers and sister when our mother and father were away at work or away for some other reason.

I'll never forget and will always be grateful for the many times my older sister Evelyn was there for us. One of the most frightening and awkward experiences a child can experience is their first day in school. My sister was there for me to help me adjust and to help me make it through that frightening day.

She was also there and would take her younger siblings like a mother hen gathers her young chicks in time of danger to safety. There were many times during the tornado season, she would either take us down the road to our grandmother's house or she would gather us in a safe corner of our old wood-frame country shotgun house until the danger had passed.

My sister Evelyn was the main and driving force that encouraged me to write this book about our family. If it had not been for her insistence and encouragement, this book would probably be nonexistent. Thank you also for being that loving older sister role model that I could look up to and being a second mother that took care of me when I could not take care of myself.

You were truly three times a lady. It was your encouragement that caused me to make many of the early positive decisions in my life. You were a great role model and left some big shoes for me to step into. Thank you for always being there when there was a family need. Thank you for the information you provided for this book about the Steadman Hays family that happened before I was old enough to remember.

I also want to thank my younger brother Dr. Greg for his contributions and for providing information about the Steadman Hays family that happened after I left home. I promise both of you, I will try to finish this book within our lifetime.

Thank you,

Evelyn!

I love you and I dedicate this book to you.

To
Some Very Special Pastors

I credit some very special pastors that have been very influential in my life. First and foremost, my father, Pastor Steadman Hays, now residing with the Lord, was the first and foremost influential pastor in my life. He instilled in me and nourished me with some very important principles early in my life. He is probably more responsible for me being who I am today than anyone else. My dad made me feel and believe that God had created me at a very special time and for a very special purpose. He created no one else to fulfill. God created me to be "the one."

Thank you,

Dad!

I look forward to seeing you again!

To
Pastor/Dr. Anthony Evans

Pastor Tony Evans has been my family pastor for more than the past thirty-five years. After struggling to finish law school, I had decided never to step foot inside another classroom again. When I first joined Oak Cliff Bible Fellowship church, I was so intrigued and impressed with his teaching and how he was able to explain and provide exegesis of the Bible in a way I had never experienced that I enrolled in Dallas Theological Seminary and took every lay class they offered.

I had been in the church all my life. As a matter of fact, being a pastor's child, I was in the church nine months before I was born. I had, like so many other faithful church attendees, been in the church but was still biblically illiterate. I had listened to a lot of sermons but still did not understand very much scripture or how that scripture applied to my life.

I will always remember one series in particular because it caused me to change the way I view myself as an attorney, a person, and the way I practice law. In the series, Dr. Evans explained that as a Christian Attorney, I was no longer just an attorney in the courtroom. I was now God's representative in the courtroom.

I try to remember and practice that every time I now step into a courtroom whether as Attorney Carl Hays or as Judge Carl Hays. Dr. Evans also did another sermon that had an impact on my career. He stated in this sermon that every Christian business owner should have a mission statement. I had never considered that before.

After almost forty years in the law profession, I now have a mission statement. My mission statement is, "It is the policy of Carl Hays Law Office to treat and represent every client the way we would want to be treated and represented and not just be their attorney but to be God's Representative in the Office and in the Court Room." Thanks to Dr. Evans, this mission statement is displayed at the entrance of my law office for all to see and read.

Thank you,

Pastor/Dr. Tony Evans!

To
Pastor/Dr. Martin E. Hawkins

My lifelong friend, my business partner, my most trusted adviser, the most compassionate, loyal, and dedicated pastor I have ever had the privilege of knowing and working with. When my wife and I first joined the then small unknown congregation, now the mega international known Oak Cliff Bible Fellowship Church—which had less than two hundred members, now with over twelve thousand members—Pastor Hawkins was one of the main reasons we joined Oak Cliff Bible Fellowship Church.

Back then, the church was divided into four home groups for special monthly home get-togethers each fourth Sunday night. Each of the four pastors would head up one of these groups in his home on each fourth Sunday night. Yes, the entire congregation/church was small enough to meet in four homes. Like most, we initially wanted to be assigned to the senior pastor's group, but God knew where he wanted us to be.

We were assigned to Pastor Hawkins's group, which turned out to be just where God wanted us to be. A special bond was created with my family that has lasted for over thirty years. I was later ordained as a deacon and served under his assistant pastor's ministry for over thirty years until Pastor Hawkins retired as assistant pastor. During those thirty-plus years serving with Pastor Hawkins, I became more convinced that my assignment was not just a random assignment but was divinely orchestrated by God.

There has never been a time in all those years when a need occurred in my family that Pastor Hawkins wasn't there. He has always been there to share in celebrations and to comfort in sorrow and times of need. He wasn't just there to offer a prayer of comfort or encouragement. I remember when my wife was hospitalized, Pastor Hawkins was there, and he also had meals catered to our home until Rhonda recovered. I am sure he had an overdemanding schedule, but that schedule was never too overdemanding for him to be there when there was a need or a celebration.

Dr. Hawkins was there when we bought and celebrated our new home. He was also there years later when my daughter Sabrina bought and celebrated her new home. He was there each time a member of the family had a medical need including being with the family at the hospital. He was there when my daughter Alana was born and also performed the wedding for my daughter Sabrina.

There has never been any occasion in my family's time of need that Pastor Hawkins wasn't there supporting us. He has given me a lot of wise counseling about many different issues over the years. He is one of the few people that I feel totally comfortable sharing my most intimate secrets with the full confidence I will receive wise counseling and my most intimate secrets will be kept confidential.

When I decided to run for district judge in Dallas County, Dr. Hawkins wasn't just my biggest financial supporter, he was there at meetings, on the phone making calls, setting up appointments, and making contact with the people that could help us win the victory, including the governor of Texas. Dr. Hawkins has advised and assisted me with every public office I have held during my political career.

The thing that impressed me most about Dr. Hawkins was his true commitment to anything and everything he took charge of. During the thirty-plus years I served under him in the assistant pastor's office, he was always committed to his calling as assistant pastor of Oak Cliff Bible Fellowship Church and to the senior pastor, Dr. Evans. He always supported and had Dr. Evans's back.

I am aware and sure there were many opportunities that came Dr. Hawkins's way that would have caused most to have abandoned the job and left for the better position, but Dr. Hawkins stayed devoted. I have often said, "Dr. Evans may have brought the visionary material to build the mega Oak Cliff Bible Fellowship Church, but Dr. Hawkins brought the compassionate glue that kept it working and kept it together."

I will never forget what Dr. Hawkins said to his staff and those of us who had been with him so long when we got the sad news that he would be retiring and leaving his position. Some members of his staff and his ministry said they would leave the church too and go with him. Most would have been flattered at such a statement of loyalty, but not Dr. Hawkins. He rebuked the ones that had made such a suggestion, and stated he was disappointed if we had been with him for so long and that was all he had taught us. His message to us was, we should be loyal and committed to the ministry and church and not to any person. "Ministry is about Christ, not about any man" (Dr. Martin E. Hawkins).

Thank you!

One of my best friends /mentor/ pastor / Dr. Martin Hawkins!

To
Pastor Carl Husband

Pastor Carl Husband, now with the Lord, was the most dedicated, spiritual, and unselfish pastor I have had the privilege of knowing. When you met Pastor Husband, you met a person that was spiritual 24-7. He was a person who did not aspire to self-greatness here on earth but to usefulness. I have never known a man that never lost focus on his purpose. He seemed to have that special purpose for which he was created. Carl Husband lived a meaningful life, a life where his focus was not on gaining earthly wealth or earthly recognition like so many ministers today but always on heavenly things above.

I went on an evangelical trip with Pastor Husband and observed some of the people he witnessed to that most would have just wiped their feet off and moved on because they appeared to be totally unconcerned and hopeless, but not Pastor Husband. When others saw hopelessness and despair, Pastor Husband saw hope and potential.

I was with Pastor Husband just a few hours before he went to be with the Lord. He had asked me to prepare his last will and testament. He was in so much pain with the cancer choking the last breath he had until I begged him to take some medication to ease the pain, but he refused because he knew the medicine might relieve the pain but would also affect his mental state. He wanted to maintain full control of his cognition and endure the pain until the end.

At times, Pastor Husband's pain was so great that his entire body would go into convulsions. It was almost unbearable for me to witness. His pains would become so intense at times until he would ask me to take a break from preparing his document to just pray for and with him to be able to endure. I believe that if the heavenly host stood at the stoning of Stephen, they most certainly had to stand when Carl Husband courageously made his transition.

During my life, I have been by the bedside of several people that have made their transition battling that dreaded illness: cancer. Most have eased their pain by using that deadly but pain-relieving drug: morphine. Carl Husband used that pain-relieving drug: faith and prayer.

Pastor Husband, in life you taught me how to live; in death you taught me how to die.

You fought a good fight, you kept the faith, you finished your course. You earned your crown.

Thank you,

Pastor Husband!

(RIP)

To

To Pastor/Dr. Larry Mercer

Pastor Larry Mercer was and has been an embodiment of all the pastors mentioned above. He has the intellect and teaching ability of Dr. Evans.

Over the years, I have had the privilege of taking many classes taught by Pastor Mercer. He is an excellent instructor. Pastor Mercer also has the compassion of Pastor Hawkins and has been there for my family as well and many other families in times of need. He has the commitment and dedication of Pastor Carl Husband. There have been many situations I have personally witnessed that would have caused most pastors to dust their shoe, pack their bags, and move on. Pastor Mercer's life, like Pastor Carl Husband's, redefined dedication and commitment.

Much of my theology and Bible knowledge is a result of having been in many classes taught by Dr. Mercer. I have used several quotes and illustrations in this book that I picked up from the teachings and sermons from him.

My life has truly been blessed and enriched by having known and experienced the life and teachings of Pastor Larry Mercer.

Thank you!

Pastor/Dr. Mercer

To
My Schoolmate and My Special Friend
Rev. Dolphus Weary

In all my years of education and having to read books, I don't ever remember reading but two books from cover to cover without putting them down, and they are Let Justice Roll Down by Rev. John Perkins and I Ain't Comin' Back by Rev. Dolphus Weary. Rev. Perkins's and Rev. Weary's books were about the life I had experienced growing up in a small town in Mississippi during some of the darkest days in America's history. I had been a disciple of Rev. John Perkins and a schoolmate of Rev. Dolphus Weary.

Rev. Weary, like me and most young Blacks growing up in Mississippi during the turbulent '60s, had but one dream—and that was to get out of Mississippi as quickly as he could and never think about going back. But Rev. Weary had a calling from God to step outside his comfort zone and return.

I admired his decision to answer God's call to step outside his comfort zone and return to Mississippi to help some people in need. That was not my calling until one day Rev. Weary put me on a guilt trip. I had heard about all the wonderful things Rev. Weary and the Mendenhall Ministry were doing and was proud to know someone was doing something good there. Rev. Weary invited me to come and view all the things headed up by the Mendenhall Ministry, which were designed to make life a little bit better for so many people living in total hopelessness and despair in my hometown.

I saw old, run-down abandoned buildings being renovated and transformed into Christian schools that provided quality education to children. I saw a law center for people who had never had access to the justice system. I saw a thrift store that provided jobs and merchandise at a price the poor could afford or even free for the needy. I saw a recreation center that provided activities for children, rather than a hangout to get in trouble.

I saw a medical center that once subjected Mississippi Black citizens the humiliation of entering the back door for basic medical needs now providing medical services for all citizens regardless of race or the ability to pay. I saw a farm that provided jobs and food for those in need. I saw a Christian community providing for people that normally would have gone without or would have been dependent on the government.

I saw a ministry that used its resources to benefit the people and not use them to build huge edifices and not using God's resources to make certain people in the ministry wealthy. I saw for the first time a vision of what I believe God's church and God's ministry should look like.

I was so impressed but still not convinced God was calling me back. I did what many will do when they feel the call but are not willing to make the commitment to step outside their comfort zone. I started making financial contributions to the ministry. Then one day I got a call from Rev. Weary. He said the ministry really appreciated my financial support but what they really needed was me.

When I had visited the ministry, I met doctors, attorneys, and other professionals from all over the country/world that were giving up their vacations and some even the whole summer to go to Mississippi to help people in need. I could no longer ease my conscience by only being willing to make a few financial contributions. I had to commit more of myself to the ministry. I answered Rev. Weary's request by stepping outside my comfort zone not to the point of returning to Mississippi permanently, because I still held dearly to Dolphus's proclamation, "I ain't coming back," but I did agree to come back routinely and become a member of the Mendenhall Ministry Board of Directors and served in the Mendenhall Ministry for several years.

Rev. Weary also, like Dr. Evans, changed the way I practice law. He and I were once discussing all the problems and hardships we had to overcome to be in the positions we were in today. Because of my experiences and hardships I had gone through in Mississippi, I had developed the attitude that if I could have made it through all the hardships, no one should have any excuses not making it. I had little pity or compassion for those who I perceived had a much better opportunity than me for becoming successful but had blown it and failed.

Rev. Weary had to remind me that although we faced a lot of hardships, poverty, and problems, but not despair because we had something more valuable than gold and silver. We had someone in our lives who believed in us, encouraged us, and taught us that there is always "a tunnel of hope through every mountain of despair."

Now because of Rev. Weary's revelation, I no longer view my clients as hopeless and worthless but as children of God who are in need of my help. Since God has blessed me to be in this position, I must use my position and God-given talents to help others. I now walk into the courtroom and take my seat of honor, whether it is as Judge Hays, presiding over a court, or as Attorney Hays representing a client. Because of Rev. Weary, I no longer view my client's seat as a seat of shame or despair but now realize that had it not been for some important people in my life who encouraged me and the grace of God, I could have very well been in the very same seat my clients find themselves in.

Thank you,

Rev. Weary!

Special Thanks and Acknowledgment to Some Other Special People

Special thanks to my wonderful niece Professor Janet Watts of Selma, Alabama; my sons-in-law Darnell Greene of Houston, Texas; Rickie Jones of Lancaster, Texas; and my friend Judge Fred "Action" Jackson of Dallas, Texas for assistance with graphics and illustrations.

I also thank my special lifelong friend Attorney B. D. Howard Jr. for constantly reminding me each day as we talk and discuss the great and eternal issues of the day. Attorney Howard and I discuss political, spiritual, and social issues almost every day. Thanks, Attorney Howard, for being my sounding board for almost forty years. We often disagree on political issues, but you always allow me to stay within my comfort zone in our disagreements. Thanks, Attorney Howard, for being there and helping to keep me spiritually accountable.

To all of Walter and Annie Hays Sr. descendants, my uncles, aunts, children, grandchildren, sisters, brothers, nieces, nephews, cousins, and beyond.

We have all been blessed to have been born into this wonderful historic Hays family. The Hays family should leave its mark in history. We have all been blessed with a special God-given talent. We have a responsibility to use the talents God has blessed us with to protect, to preserve, and to pass on the wonderful Walter Hays family legacy. If we don't, the rich Hays family history will be dumped in the historical trash bins of time. I have tried to set the wheel in motion by laying the historical foundation. What contribution will you leave?

Thanks,

Walter and Annie Hays Sr. Family.

II

Foreword

Gregory L. Hays, MD
President, CEO, Hays Innovations
Senior Staff Physician
Assistant Director, Division of Emergency Ultrasound
Henry Ford Hospital, Detroit, Michigan (ret.)
Assistant Clinical Professor
Wayne State University, School of Medicine (ret.)
Adjunct Clinical Professor
University of Michigan, School of Medicine (ret.)

Sometime during the fall of 1997, as I drove to the airport to catch a flight to Vancouver, Canada, to attend the world's largest conference on the treatment of sepsis, I found myself reflecting on the events that had led me to that point in my life. Not only was I attending the conference, but I was giving a lecture on some cutting-edge research that was being done at our hospital—research that would ultimately change how sepsis was handled the world over.

The recent step that had led me there was immediately clear, which was my association with a mentor who was a visionary and who was about to change the practice of medicine worldwide. Because of the work that we were doing at the time, he later became renowned as the foremost leader in sepsis care. Things were just starting to heat up, and there was a lot of interest in our work, so because of his scheduling demands, I was afforded the opportunity to stand in for my mentor at this conference.

As I reflected that day, I soon recognized that beyond this immediate link in the winding chain of my life, there had been a more foundational pathway on the long road from the Jim Crow South to the podium where I would be addressing global leaders in medicine. Navigating this tricky path had taken more than just the determination of the single man, and as I traveled, lost in thought, I recognized the benefactors who had been so instrumental in my success.

Indeed, the path that I found myself following had been blazed by several others including my siblings, all of whom are older than me and all of whom had found their own paths out of the oppression that was designed to hold them down. There had also been my father who, in his youth, had been denied an education himself but who had pointed us all toward higher education as a means of escaping the tragic destiny that befell so many Southern Blacks.

In my contemplation of the past, my thoughts went to one trailblazer in particular who had most influenced me as a child: the author of When God Calls You Out of Your Comfort Zone and a man who I am proud to call my big brother, Judge Carl Hays. I clearly remember Carl leaving our modest house in Mississippi in 1966, heading off to college, and I also remember being reminded daily of how I was expected to follow his example. From this point forward for me, attending college was no longer a possibility but an inevitability.

Later, his entry into law school coincided with the beginnings of desegregation in our small town. This timing was extremely important because many of the town's citizens, including some teachers, were violently opposed to the new social circumstance in which they found themselves. Consequently, there were overt efforts to ensure the failure of what they viewed as a social experiment and an upheaval of their way of life. I, however, always knew that despite the not-so-subtle messages to the contrary, I could be successful in whatever career path I chose to follow. I knew that if my brother could make it, so could I. Upon realizing the important role that he had played in my life, I picked up the phone that fall day and made a call to thank my older brother for being the tool that I needed when God called me out of my comfort zone.

When God Calls You Out of Your Comfort Zone is a very thoughtfully written contemplative look at one man's journey against the odds as he struggled to succeed despite a social network constructed to prevent the success of its black citizens. The author skillfully identifies the points during his struggle where the tools needed for his success were provided by God. He challenges the readers to look beyond their immediate struggles and identify the tools that are being provided and to use those tools to create success in their lives. Historical reference is provided by analogizing the plights of several iconic biblical characters such as Noah and Jonah and observing how, in their darkest moments, these characters relied upon their faith to find the pathway that God had provided to lead them out of peril. The author provides an inspiring account of the triumphs and trials of his biggest hero, our father, as he fought to protect himself, his family, and his property in a hostile and sometimes violent environment while inspiring his family and the community to higher ideals.

It was through faith, courage, and perseverance that our father, a small-town pastor, discovered the pathway that God had provided for him. That pathway allowed him to accomplish two of his most sacredly held tasks: leadership of his community in their endeavor to attain civil rights and the provision of a roadmap for success for his children.

Although When God Calls You Out of Your Comfort Zone is about one man's struggle, it is everyone's story. Anyone who has found himself in a seemingly untenable circumstance can draw upon the wisdom imparted through the historical examples and clear extrapolations provided by the author. Fostering the courage to move out of our comfort zones is essential for success in life, and this insightful account provides inspiration and a new perspective on courage and faith.

To the discerning reader, the following pages are a gold mine of wisdom and provide vital keys to understanding how to recognize "Noah's boat" in a storm. I am greatly honored to provide this foreword, and I hope that the reader will benefit from the wisdom of Judge Hays as much as I have over the years.

III
Introduction

The Scripture gives many illustrations and examples where and how God sometimes calls for his followers to step outside their comfort zone on faith (walk by faith, not by sight [2 Cor. 5:7]) into situations that are not very comfortable to accept or understand. We are sometimes called upon by the Lord to remove ourselves from our daily routine and journey to places or situations that make no sense to our thinking or rationale at the time. God called Abram, "Go from your country, your people and your father's household to the land I will show you" (Genesis 12:1).

Abram was willing to step outside his comfort zone and obey God, and God made him the father of a great nation. Jonah was not willing to step outside his comfort zone and disobeyed God, so God called a fish and Jonah was swallowed up by that fish.

Sometimes we are given the opportunity to make the choice, and sometimes we have no say-so in the decision. Dr. Tony Evans, senior pastor of the Oak Cliff Bible Fellowship Church in Dallas, Texas, in one of his series, refers to these as "detours to our God-given destinies."

How men and women have responded to these detours in many cases have changed and set the course of history. Some have accepted their call, and some have tried to run away or avoid God's call to step outside their comfort zone, such as Jonah. When Jonah was called upon by the Lord to step outside his comfort zone and go to Nineveh to preach, he did not want to obey God's call and tried to run away from God's presence.

Jonah, like so many of us today, was afraid to step outside of his comfort zone and obey God. He attempted to run from the call of God and refused to perform what God had called him to do. The results of his resistance to the call of God should serve as an example of how it is impossible to run from God. Jonah only needed the wisdom of David, who said, "If I ascend up to the heavens, you are there; if I make my bed in hell, you are there" (Ps. 139:8).

We, too, could learn a lot and avoid many problems if we understood the wisdom of David. When we understand we cannot run or resist the call of God, we can avoid a lot of unnecessary problems. When Jonah refused to answer the call of the Lord, all hell broke loose. His life and the lives of those around him were all in turmoil. When Jonah finally answered the call of God and obeyed, a whole nation was saved.

God has a unique call, purpose, and time for all his creation to respond. We all have a Nineveh calling. Just as in (Matt. 25:14) the parable of the talents. God has given each person talents according to each person's ability. God gave Esther a talent of beauty. It is reported that Esther was one of the most beautiful women that ever lived. Mordecai had to remind Esther that her beauty was a talent given by God to be used for a time such as these. Esther used her talent to save her people.

We can see throughout human history and most certainly in biblical history how God generally called and used people who were willing to step outside their comfort zone to accomplish his will. It is important to recognize and be willing to step outside the comfort zone to be used by God.

God has given each one of his children a special and unique talent. One day God will call forth each one of his children to give an account for their special and unique talent. Will you say, "God, I was afraid to step outside my comfort zone and use the talent you gave me"? Will God's response be, "Well done, my good and faithful servant," or will it be, "Depart from me you wicked and slothful servant" (Matt. 25:14)?

If we fail to use the talent God has given us, God will remove the talent and give it to someone else. "So, take the talent from him and give it to him who has ten" (Matt. 26:29).

People are generally fearful and reluctant to step outside their comfort zone just as the servant in Matthew 26 because of what others may think or say or how others will feel about them. It is more important what God thinks about us rather than what people think about us. Sometime people fear they are not qualified. "God does not call the qualified; God qualifies the ones he calls" (Dr. Larry Mercer).

People also fear what may happen to them and their family. Most of all, people fear criticism and how others may respond to them. Every person that will be mentioned in this book had to face constant criticism. Criticism is one of the main reasons for people not stepping outside their comfort zone to be used by God.

In this book, we will mainly chronicle the life and works of my dad, Steadman Hays, by researching his historical roots shortly after slavery and how God called and used him at a very special and unique time in human history to step outside his comfort zone to perform a special and unique purpose. We will examine the lives and calls of a few biblical characters first and show how the Bible recorded their response to God's call.

We will then examine the lives of some of the characters and events during the American civil rights era that had a big impact on the life and call of my dad, Steadman Hays, to step outside his comfort zone at a very treacherous and dangerous time in American history.

We will also show how God has, throughout human history, called and used ordinary people to accomplish extraordinary feats by keeping the faith and stepping outside their comfort zone when necessary to accomplish God's will for their lives.

We will first examine the lives of biblical personalities like Noah, an ordinary man who had no idea how to overcome the great catastrophe of the flood and had never even seen rain, but because Noah was willing to listen and be obedient to God's Word and step outside his comfort zone, God said, "I have a boat for you."

This book and the story of Noah are for those that feel the floods of life are about to crush in on them and they can't see a way out. God has a boat for you too, but you must be willing to listen to God, keep the faith, and step outside your comfort zone if necessary to realize that when the floods of life come, God has a boat for you too.

Just as we will see how God provided a boat for Noah, we will see how God provided a ram for Abraham, a rod for Moses, a stone for David, a palace for Esther, a fish for Jonah, a testimony for Peter, a Resurrection for Jesus, a destiny fulfilled for Paul, and a crown for all who are willing to step outside their comfort zone to accomplish God's will.

In many cases people are engulfed and drown because they miss the boat—miss out on opportunities because they didn't see the ram in the bush, as did Abraham. They can't cross troubled waters because they don't know how to use their rod of God like Moses. They are defeated because they couldn't find their stone like David. Many miss out because they are reluctant to step outside their comfort zone, trust, listen, and understand God's mission for their lives.

We will also examine the lives of some modern-day characters who changed the course of history by listening, trusting, and stepping outside their comfort zone to accomplish God's will for their lives and the lives of others—people like Harriet Tubman, who became free from the cruelty of slavery but had a God-called mission to return to free others by leading them to freedom with her Underground Railroad; Rosa Parks was denied a seat on a segregated bus but answered her godly call and took a stand so many could have a seat; Medgar Evers was denied equality but answered his godly call and gave his life for the equality of all; Dr. Martin Luther King Jr., whom God gave a dream to share with a nation; Malcolm X, who tried to give an identity to a people that had their identity stolen; and my dad Steadman Hays, who, like many other African Americans of his day, were denied many of the basic opportunities afforded to American citizens, answered his godly call by inspiring his children and others to never give up on the vision of being all God created them to be.

Little did these people probably know that they may have been created at their special and unique time in history to be called by God to step outside their comfort zone, just as Mordecai stated to Esther, "for a time such as these" (Esther 4). God had a unique reason, a unique purpose, and a unique time for creating each one of his children.

In this book, we will see how God was able to provide a railroad at a unique time for Harriet Tubman; a seat at a unique time for Rosa Parks; a dream at a unique time for Dr. Martin Luther King Jr.; a new vision at a unique time for Medgar Evers; a new identity at a unique time for Black people for Malcolm X; "the one" at a unique time for Steadman Hays.

These people were only able to accomplish their victories because they were willing to disregard the dangers and criticism they faced and were willing to step outside their comfort zone to answer their godly call.

Finally, we will examine the church, God's house of prayer, today in hopes of exposing how many false prophets have gone out into the world just as the Bible predicted would happen in the last days to try to deceive and mislead God's people (Matt. 24:11).

The Bible predicted that most will be deceived and misled by these false prophets. We will try to expose how in many church worship services today, the false prophets have infiltrated the church worship service with satanic rituals, while most are deceived, just as the Bible predicted, into believing they are truly worshipping God (Matt. 24:36).

We will see how most Bible prophecies have already been fulfilled and other Bible prophecies are being fulfilled right before our eyes in the way we live, the way we worship, and the way we follow blindly after these false prophets just as the Bible predicted.

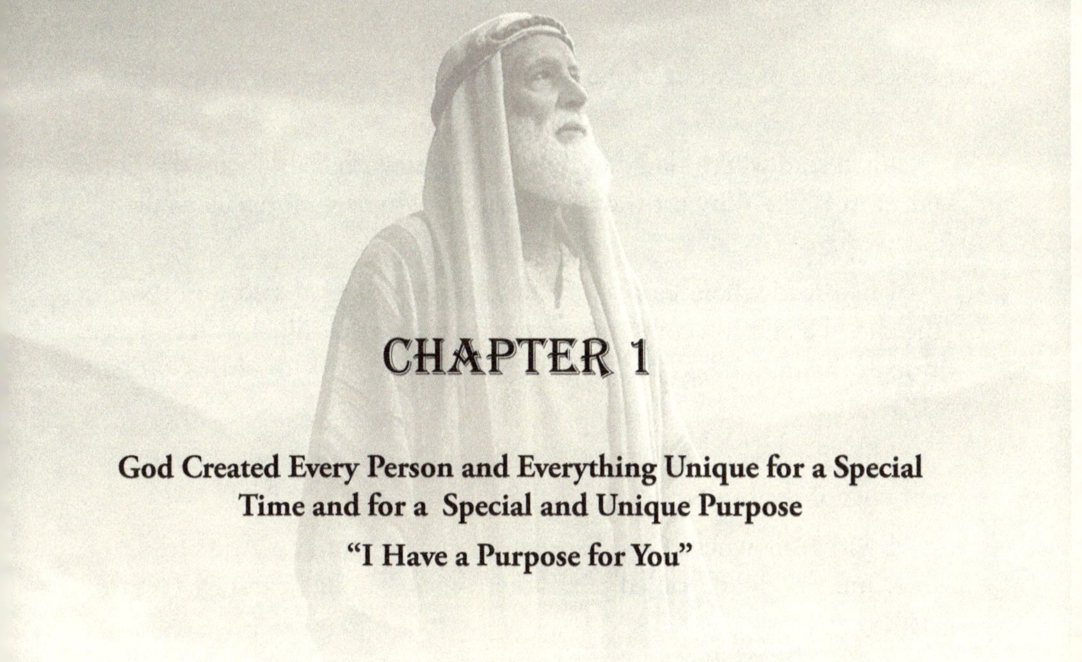

CHAPTER 1

God Created Every Person and Everything Unique for a Special Time and for a Special and Unique Purpose

"I Have a Purpose for You"

In order to understand our call and special, unique purpose for being created by God, we must understand his call and learn how to communicate with God. "We were all created on purpose for a purpose by God," said Dr. Larry Mercer. God calls and uses people through circumstances, visions, and most importantly, the Holy Spirit to communicate with us today. Before Jesus's death, he told his depressed, bewildered, and fearful disciples to fear not for he would send the Holy Ghost to be with them. The Holy Ghost was sent and is today available with a host of angelic angels for us all.

During my early years, I was having a real difficult time understanding my call and what my purpose in life was and what God had created me for because I didn't know how to communicate with God. There are millions and millions of people all over the world, but you and I were created at a very special time, unique and different than any other person God created. If we were created unique and different, it should then follow that we were also created for a unique and special purpose. Understanding your uniqueness and purpose requires understanding how to communicate with God.

I had read how God had communicated with many people throughout the Bible. I had read where God had communicated with Adam when God told Adam, "Of every tree of the garden thou mayest freely eat; But of the tree of the knowledge of good and evil" (Gen. 2:16–17).

I had read where God had communicated with Cain: "And the Lord said unto Cain; Why art thou wroth? And why is countenance fallen?" (Gen. 4:6).

I had read where God spoke to Noah: "And God said unto Noah, 'The end of all flesh is come before me; for the earth is filled with violence through them; and, behold, I will destroy them with the earth'" (Gen. 6:13).

I had read where God spoke to Moses: "God called unto him out of the midst of the bush, and said 'Moses, Moses' (Exodus 3:4).

I had read where God had spoken unto Samuel: "And the Lord came, and stood, and called as at other times, Samuel, Samuel" (1 Sam. 3:10).

I had read where God had communicated with David: "Therefore David inquired of the Lord, saying, 'Shall I go and smite the Philistines?' And the Lord said unto David, 'Go, and smite the Philistines, and save Keilah'" (1 Sam. 23:2).

I had read where God had communicated with the apostle Paul: "And as he journeyed, he came near Damascus: and suddenly there shined round about him a light from heaven: And he fell to the earth, and heard a voice saying unto him, 'Saul, Saul, why persecutest thou me?'" (Acts 9:3–4).

As a young boy, I was brought up in the church and had been taught that God speaks to his people today just as he talked to them in biblical days. I so badly wanted God to speak to me in my times of question, despair, and trouble, but he never did, at least I didn't recognize when he did try to communicate with me. One day I went way down in the back woods of my grandfather's pasture to be alone and asked God to speak to me, but he never did. I soon gave up on that request.

I hadn't been taught and didn't know or understand at the time that God spoke directly to his people in the Old Testament. Jesus, "The Word," became flesh and made his dwelling among us, came, and spoke directly to us while incarnated on earth (John 1:14), and when Jesus ascended, Jesus sent the Holy Spirit to dwell among and speak to us. I was confused and didn't know how to communicate with the Holy Spirit.

Years later, after graduating from a Bible college, law school and after having studied the Bible for many years and having been in the church almost every Sunday for most of my life and being a pastor's son (I was even in church nine months before I was born), I still did not understand how to communicate with God.

Then one morning I was driving in my car headed to a routine day in court when I heard this preacher explaining how to listen to God. I had my radio tuned to one of the Christian stations that I often listen to when I heard Dr. Charles Stanley expound on a series, "Listening to God."

In the series, Dr. Stanley explained how God communicates with us today. I was so impressed with Dr. Stanley's explanation that I ordered the whole series. Since then I have used it hundreds of times for personal use as well as to counsel my clients. Thanks, Dr. Stanley! I now better recognize God's voice and have a much better understanding of how God communicates with us today.

Now I know God has always been trying to communicate with me all along. I just didn't recognize his voice and how he was trying to communicate with me. "My sheep hear my voice and I know them, and they follow me" (John 10:27–30). God promised he would never leave us nor forsake us (Heb. 13:5). If God is with us, he must also communicate to us.

Communicating with God

Radio and television waves are all around us, but if we don't have a radio or television receiver, we can't receive the radio or television waves. Radios and televisions send out electromagnetic radiation with wavelengths in electromagnetic spectrum that can only be received by a receiver. God is omnipresent but in the spirit realm; therefore, in order to communicate with God, we must have our spiritual receiver tuned into God's frequencies.

Sometimes God uses other people to speak to us. The Scripture teaches us that there are angels all around us. Andy Griffin illustrated it best in a beautiful emotional Christmas poem "The Christmas Guest." In one of my favorite Christmas poems, Andy Griffin tells the story of an old man who had spent many Christmases alone with no family or friends because all had died, but on this special Christmas, he had a vision in a dream that God was coming to be his Christmas guest.

The man, in preparation for his special guest, cleaned, polished, and did everything around the house and got ready for his special guest. As night approached, God had not shown up. Then the man heard a knock at his door. He rushed to the door thinking it was God, but it was only a poor old beggar cold and hungry. The man invited the old beggar in, fed him, and allowed him to get warm by his fire and gave him some shoes for his cold feet. After the beggar left, the man was still waiting on God, when he heard another knock at his door. The man again rushed to the door hoping it was God, but again it was only an old lady cold and hungry. The man invited her in, fed and gave her a cup of tea, and allowed her to warm herself in front of his fire.

After the lady left, the man became worried that maybe God was not coming because it was getting late, then he heard a cry in the darkness. The man opened his door, only to find a lost child. He took the child in, and after allowing her to warm herself, he helped the child find her way home.

When the man returned to his own home, he was overcome with sadness because he knew Christmas was nearly over and God had not come as he said he would to be his Christmas guest. Before lying down, the old man prayed and asked God why he had not come as he said he would.

God answered and said, "I did come! Three times I came to your lonely door and three times you invited me in. I was the man with the cold feet. I was the woman you gave something to eat. I was the lost child on the lonely street. Three times I knocked at your door, and three times I was your Christmas guest."

The story makes you wonder, how many times has God or one of his angels been our guest and we did not recognize them (Heb. 13:2)? Did we respond the way the old man did and invited them in, or did we turn away God when he came to our door to be our guest?

I can't say I have always heard, recognized, and understood when God was trying to communicate with me, but I can unequivocally say there have been many times God has communicated with me as clear as if he were sitting right next to me. Sometimes God will try to communicate to me that the fire is hot, but other times because of my disobedience and my not being able to pick up his spiritual wavelengths, God will let me get burned by the fire in order to hear him.

Satan also exists and communicates in the spiritual realm. But since Satan is the prince of this world and since Adam gave this world to Satan, man is born in sin and is born with his sin nature with his receiver already on the same spiritual frequencies to communicate with Satan. We are all born with a sin nature and the ability to communicate on the sin frequency but must be taught how to tune in on God's spiritual frequency. Some say this is the reason why we lie.

One time I was most certainly tuned in on God's spiritual frequency and God clearly spoke to me. It really stood out because I was in a disagreement with the deacon board that I served on at Oak Cliff Bible Fellowship in Dallas, Texas. We were expanding our church. I disagreed with the expansion unless we could build more parking spaces for the members we already had.

Our church, Oak Cliff Bible Fellowship, with our young dynamic expository Bible teaching pastor Dr. Anthony "Tony" Evans, had grown from about two hundred members to several thousands, and we desperately needed more parking space. We were a young church with a lot of young mothers and young children that had grown so fast because of this new style of preaching that most African-Americans were not accustomed to.

Many expecting mothers without adequate parking space still flocked to this church even though they had to walk some distance to get to the church in all kinds of weather every Sunday and even on most Wednesday nights. The neighborhood was also a concern for women to be walking alone at night.

My wife was also a young mother with small children, and I was speaking and taking a stand for them too. I was overruled and the building expansion went on without new parking space. I would get so upset when I saw my wife having to walk a long distance, as well as other young mothers with their small children, to get to church because there were not enough parking spaces closer to the church.

Many times, I would drop my family off in front of the church, drive a few blocks down the street, and walk back to the church because there were not adequate parking spaces to accommodate the constantly fast-growing congregation. On this particular Sunday morning, I was especially angry as I walked to church because it was raining and cold. I had gotten soaking wet walking in the cold rain to get to our church.

My anger had given the devil a straight line of communication with me. While we may sometimes have trouble communicating with God, the devil will seize the opportunity and will communicate with us. The devil was in control of the conversation with all kinds of negative thoughts going through my head.

Just as I arrived at the entrance door to the church, my anger grew even more because I was so wet, cold, and did not feel like being in church and the devil had taken advantage of the situation. God had this car suddenly pull into one of the few handicap parking spaces at the church's entrance. I noticed as the driver got out of this car, he went to open up the trunk of the car. I then observed him retrieve a wheelchair from the trunk and went around to the passenger's side.

I watched him help lift out of the car a man who had no legs. What a message! I heard God loud and clear speak to me. "Here you are complaining about having to walk a few blocks and this man wished he could be in your shoes so that he could just be able to walk."

God's message was unquestionably real and clear. For once I was tuned in on the same wave frequency and God was able to clearly communicate to me. It also gave me a sermon and message to pass on to others. I often meet people who are depressed and complaining about their various situations. I let them know that there are people praying to be in their situation or in their shoes.

I tell them, "Your shoes are not at the hospital this morning, nor the jail house or even the funeral home." People generally get the message and have a positive response and will thank me for reminding them of just how blessed they really are, that regardless of their situation, there are others wishing they could be in their shoes.

Sometimes God puts us in situations and have us go through things so that we can learn and be a blessing to others. Having to walk in the rain and cold to church gave me the opportunity to understand how God communicated to me through an impaired man and the message he wanted me to pass on to others. That disabled man probably did not even know that God was using him to communicate a message to me that I could communicate to others. Sometimes God uses us without us even knowing.

There have been so many times in my personal life where God has clearly called and communicated with me. There were times I did not recognize God's voice or understand what he was trying to communicate to me. Sometimes God has to allow me to feel the pain of the flames in order to get my attention. But as I grow more spiritual, his communication becomes easier for me to understand.

We must also learn that just as God speaks to us, so does Satan. Satan has always wanted to be like God. That is why Satan was kicked out of heaven (Rev. 12:7–12). Satan first appeared and communicated with Eve in the Garden of Eden. Just like it is important to recognize the voice of God, it is important to be able to discern and recognize the voice of Satan.

Satan will control our thinking and what we do if we don't recognize his voice and his deception. Many of the mistakes we make in life are because Satan has spoken to us and we failed to recognize his voice and did things based on what Satan had influenced us to do.

Just as I had the experience in communicating with God with the man that had no feet and could not walk, there have been times in my life I clearly recognized the voice of Satan. One clear example was when Dr. Hawkins had appointed my wife, Rhonda, and me to be care cell leaders over a small group in our church. Each fourth Sunday afternoon, we would either meet at our home or go to one of the other group members' home to have prayer and Bible study.

It seemed to never fail that every fourth Sunday, just before we were preparing for Bible study, my wife and I would have some disagreement over some small, insignificant issue like my wife complaining about what I was wearing or my complaining about my wife being late. These were small, insignificant issues but just enough to cause disruption and distraction, which interfered just enough to keep us from being totally focused on our roles as spiritual leaders.

Satan was able to continue his communication until one fourth Sunday, just as my wife and I were preparing to leave our home and go lead the prayer and Bible study at another group members' home, Satan spoke to me and told me to complain to my wife that she was late again.

This time I was able to recognize Satan's voice. Normally, I would not have recognized his voice and would have followed through with creating this disruption with my wife, which would have caused us to have been less effective spiritual leaders, which was the goal of Satan.

After I recognized Satan's voice and what he was trying to do, I told my wife, "Before we go to this care cell meeting today, we need to pray and get ourselves spiritually ready." I never witnessed the truth of Scripture as I did that day: "Resist the Devil and he will flee from you" (James 4:7), for we had one of the best care cell meetings and we never had that problem with Satan again because we were able to recognize Satan's voice and how to resist him and he fled just as the scripture had said.

Many of the problems we face today are because we don't recognize the voice of Satan and what he is trying to do through us. Satan is a spiritual being and can only be defeated spiritually. Man is not able to defeat a spiritual being but must as Jesus did use the Scripture (Matt. 4:1–11). We can overcome Satan and resolve many of the problems we face if we learn how to recognize the voice of Satan and how to use scripture to resist him.

I hope and pray that after reading and understanding how God communicates and has created each one of us uniquely and at a special time with a unique and special purpose that more people will be willing to step outside their comfort zone and attempt to learn how to communicate with God so they may understand their unique purpose and how to fulfill it. Rick Warren explained it best in his book The Purpose-Driven Life.

Many are afraid to step outside their comfort zone to answer the call of God and accomplish what God created them for because of insecurity and discouraging signals from Satan. When we don't understand how God is trying to speak to us, Satan will. Some will not use the talents God has given them because they fear being inadequate and unqualified. Dr. Larry Mercer of the Oak Cliff Bible Fellowship Church in Dallas, Texas, recently stated in one of his sermons, "God does not call the qualified; God qualifies the ones he calls."

Dr. Mercer's definition for whom God calls makes us all qualified to answer the call of God, because according to Dr. Mercer, God will qualify the ones he calls. "God's call is not based on our suitability but on our availability" (Dr. Larry Mercer).

Many times, we waste time vacillating over what God has called us to do. God created each one of his children unique at a special time for a special purpose. God created some of his children stronger physically than others, some bigger than others, some smarter than others, but the one thing God gave all his creation an equal portion of is time.

The poorest man has just as much time as the richest. The richest man in the world with all his wealth cannot buy one second of time. We should therefore use our time well. We should not "sleep-walk through life" (Dr. Larry Mercer). We should also remember, "lost time can never be found."

In the Bible, the book of Genesis records the life of Methuselah as having lived longer than any other man. The book of Genesis states that Methuselah lived 969 years, and that is about all that is written about Methuselah. The Gospel books record the life of another man that only lived on earth about thirty-three years. Jesus only lived about thirty-three years on earth as a man, and all the Bible is written about him. Therefore, it's not how long one lives that matters; it's what one does while he lives. We need to therefore take full advantage of our God-given talents and the time God has given us to use them.

I wrote the following poem about how we sometimes misuse our God-given time by making plans but never putting dates on those plans. We sometime miss out on the most important things in life because we don't take advantage of the time that God has given us and use it wisely. The poem is titled "We'll Keep In Touch."

We'll Keep In Touch
by
Carl Hays

I saw my little friend today,
As she came outside with me to play.
We were so full of joy and not one care.
We thought we were the inseparable pair.
And the wind blew, and the flowers grew;
We made plans, like we often do—
Plans that too often never come true.
At the end of the day, we bided goodbye.
But we'll keep in touch as time passes by.
Yes! We'll keep in touch as time passes by.

And then the day came, and we are off to school.
Our pencils, our papers, and our sliding rule.
Our days in school seem to go by so slow.
We just couldn't wait to graduate and exit the door.
And the wind blew, and the flowers grew.
We made plans, like we often do—
Plans that too often never come true.
But we'll keep in touch as time passes by.
Yes! We'll keep in touch as time passes by.
Then off to college, she went her way and I went mine,
Never giving one thought to the passing time.
I made new friends and I'm sure she did too.
It's so strange what time and separation can do.
We eventually lost contact through the passing years.
For we were both so busy with our newfound peers.
And the wind blew, and the flowers grew.
We made plans, like we often do—
Plans that too often never come true.
But we stay in touch as time passes by.
Yes! We'll stay in touch as time passes by.
Then I got a call, my friend was terminally ill and hospitalized.
I dropped everything and rushed to be at her side.
But when I saw her, I knew she would pass any day.
With over a million words, I could find none to say.

For her I knew the flowers were gone and the wind had blown.
And it wouldn't be long before my friend was gone.
But we promised to keep in touch, but time passed us by.
Yes! We'll keep in touch, but time passed us by.

The poem was inspired by the many precious, happy, and sad memories of my loving cousin Celestine Hays. Celestine and I had grown up together in a small town in Mississippi. We had attended elementary, junior high, and high school together and, as the poem states, made a lot of plans to keep in touch for the rest of our lives.

After finishing high school, we left our hometown to go off to college and to pursue our careers. We kept in touch for a few years and would see each other and visit when we were home on semester breaks. As the years passed, we let our new friends, families, and careers become more important than our promises to keep in touch. It was our plan to keep in touch, but we let time pass us by.

Years later, I got a letter from a family member informing me that Celestine was very sick and was not expected to live. Unlike the poem states, I never got a chance to see my little friend, because by the time I received the letter, Celestine had already died and had been funeralized. The real pain came when I received a copy of her obituary and saw where Celestine had requested that I be included as a pallbearer and was listed as one in her funeral program.

We had grown up together and had planned to always be that inseparable pair, to keep in touch, but at Celestine's most important moment in life or death, I was too busy being out of the country and didn't even get her family's letter until after she was buried. I will now have to live with and carry the memory of letting my job, my career, and new adventures become more important than the things that should be the most important in life: family and friends.

As stated earlier, God created each one of his children at a special time with a special and unique talent to perform a special and unique purpose during our short lives on earth. Many of us get so busy with jobs, careers, and chasing the mighty dollar until we miss out on the most important things in life and what we were created for.

I never got a chance to know very much about Celestine or her family after we grew up because I was too busy with my jobs and career.

I did appreciate her family, and I was deeply honored by being included as one of her honorary pallbearers. I am thankful my cousin and I were still friends to the very end even though our lives had taken us down different roads. I guess I should have taken counsel in the following verse: "Yet you do not know what your life will be like tomorrow. You are just like a vapor that appears for a little while and then vanishes away" (James 4:14).

Celestine, RIP.

CHAPTER 2

God Calls Noah

God Has a Boat for You

One of the most difficult, awkward, and unpleasant things for one to do is to be called upon to step outside their comfort zone. Most people feel very comfortable just being ordinary and doing ordinary things. Most people like the recognition and the attention of fame and greatness but feel very uncomfortable and are unwilling to step outside their comfort zone and make the sacrifice to accomplish fame and greatness. Most people take the Zebedee brothers' approach to greatness: "Give it to me not based on my personal sacrifice or my personal willingness to step outside my comfort zone to accomplish greatness, but give it to me because of who I am or whom I know."

After Jesus gave sight to the blind, fed the hungry, and raised the dead, everyone wanted to be his friend and follow him. But when Jesus asked, "Do you see what I see?" (the cross), they all fell back including the twelve. When it comes to making a sacrifice or stepping outside the comfort zone, most people would rather remain just an unseen figure in the crowd. These people very seldom accomplish anything extraordinary or special and fail to reach their God-given purpose in life.

Just as God created each snowflake, each grain of sand, each leaf on a tree, etc., different and with a different and unique purpose, God created each person different and unique with a special and unique gift and purpose in life. That is why there should not be any racism. When one dislikes a person because of the color of their skin or the texture of their hair or any other physical difference, then he is telling God he did not know what he was doing in creating that person different.

In the Bible as well as in human history there are many illustrations where ordinary people have been called upon to step outside their comfort zone to do extraordinary things, either because of their circumstances or because of their faith. These people have shaped and influenced our lives and made a difference in the world.

Throughout the Bible, God called on ordinary people to perform extraordinary feats. In the book of Genesis, when God decided the world had become too wicked for him to allow mankind to continue to violate his statutes and morality, God decided to destroy the world, but God needed one man to step outside his comfort zone to make a difference and to preserve mankind.

Noah was that man. What was so spectacular about what Noah did was what is generally spectacular about what every person must do when they are called out of their comfort zone. They must in many cases face the unknown and be willing, as the song writer wrote, to "reach the unreachable star, fight the unbeatable foe, bear with unbearable sorrow, and go where the brave dare not go." These are a few of the characteristics of people who are willing to step outside their comfort zone to make a difference.

God told Noah that he was going to destroy the world, but he wanted him to step outside his comfort zone so that mankind would be preserved. God told Noah he was going to destroy the world by raining water from heaven. What made this so difficult for the ordinary man to understand was, it had never rained before. Man had no knowledge of rain. Noah had no knowledge of rain but had to step out on faith because he did not know what rain was. Noah, like Abraham, was told he would have a son at a hundred years old, and Mary was told she would have a son even though she was a virgin. All had to face the unknown.

God gave Noah the specifications for building an ark for his family and the selected animal kingdom that God wanted to preserve to replenish the earth. The fact that God already knew how many people Noah would be able to convert after forty years of preaching creates the question of predestination versus free will. If we were all predestined, would God have had to send his son into the world to be crucified for us to be saved? It is a complicated theological issue that needs a lot of explanation.

Sometimes we read and hear about these extraordinary people and what they did to change the course of history without really understanding the sacrifices, ridicule, struggles, and hardships they might have faced. Noah didn't just step out one day and build an ark and call out the animals and that's the end of the story. It took much work and many years of criticism and humiliation from his neighbors, friends, and the people that saw this old man building an ark on dry land and preaching about it's going to rain. The book of Genesis does not state specifically how many years it took to complete the ark. Noah and his family spent another year and seventeen days aboard the ark during and after the flood.

It is difficult to explain the unknown. During Noah's ministry people did not know what rain was. It had never rained in human history. People generally ridicule and fear the unknown. The scripture does not state specifically how long Noah preached about the oncoming flood or how many years it took to build the ark. Some biblical scholars believe it was about 127 years. They all agree that Noah preached the same sermon during that time, "It's going to rain." Noah was apparently a great ark builder but was not quite as successful in his ministry, for after preaching 120 years, he did not produce one convert outside his family. But Noah accomplished God's purpose and plan for him. Noah and his three sons would replenish the world.

How We Can Apply the Story of Noah

God needs boat builders today. God has a job for you. There will come the floods in our lives, but just as God warned Noah and asked him to warn the people of the impending flood, God's Word has warned us about the impending floods that are facing us. "Man born of a woman is of a few days and full of trouble" (Job 14:1). The story of Noah demonstrates God's love and how he will provide for those that are obedient to his word, but it also demonstrates God's wrath for those that are disobedient.

The flood destroyed everything—all mankind, women, children, babies, cats, dogs, chickens, and all live form. The flood should demonstrate man should always seek God's blessings but should always try to avoid God's wrath. God is a merciful God but will when necessary impose his wrath.

The story of Noah should warn and prepare for the impending floods of our lives. Sometimes our flood may be the flood of finances, and the bill collectors seem to be about to engulf us. Sometimes it may be the flood of depression and it appears we have nowhere to turn. Sometimes it may be the flood of loneliness and you have looked for love in all the wrong places. Sometimes it may be the flood of illness and the doctors and medical professionals have no hope and are ready to pull the flood sheet over your head.

We must learn from Noah to trust God. Even though it may appear we don't understand, we must trust God's Word. Neither Noah nor anyone else during his lifetime had ever seen rain. And after 120 years of preaching "It's going to rain," people probably thought Noah was a nut. But Noah kept faithful to God's Word and kept right on preaching, "It's going to rain."

In the story of Noah, God has a message for you. When the storms and floods of life are emerging at your door and about to engulf you, if you are faithful and obedient to God's Word, that message is,

"God has a boat for you."

First Corinthians 10:13: God did not promise floods would not come in our lives. He did promise he understood just how much we could bear and his faithfulness in that he would never send more floods in our lives than the faithful could bear. And with the flood, he would provide a way out, "a boat"! So when you see a friend or family member appearing to be overwhelmed with the problems of life, tell them God wants them to step outside their comfort zone on faith because

"God has a boat for you."

CHAPTER 3

God Calls Abraham

"I Have a Ram for You"

Abraham was another character in the book of Genesis God called upon to step out in faith and outside his comfort zone to accomplish God's will in his life. Abraham is one of the best illustrations of how God can take and use an ordinary person with all the weaknesses and lack of courage and use them to accomplish extraordinary ordeals.

Abraham was a coward, a liar, and even a man like Adam who allowed his wife to influence him to disobey God, but God was still able to take this weak lying coward and make him the father of a nation. God could use Abraham because he was willing to step outside his comfort zone to be used by God.

Abraham did not always demonstrate that unquestionable faith. He was willing to trust God in sacrificing his son Isaac. Abraham was an ordinary man with ordinary weaknesses. He even led his enemies to believe that Sarah, his wife, was really his sister. This was to avoid possibly being killed so that his enemies could take his wife. Sarah was in fact Abraham's half sister, but he did not tell them that Sarah was his wife.

Abraham also demonstrated weakness and lack of faith when God promised him he would make him the father of a great nation by allowing his wife, Sarah, to influence him into having a baby with Sarah's maidservant Hagar. Abraham and Sarah's decision to try to help God created a problem, like Adam, that still exists to this day.

Abraham did, however, demonstrate tremendous faith and the willingness to step outside his comfort zone to trust and obey God. God had instructed Abraham to leave his home and go to an unknown land. Abraham trusted and obeyed. When Abraham and his nephew Lot could no longer camp together, he allowed Lot to select the part of the land he wanted to settle in. Lot naturally selected what he could see as the best, which included Sodom and Gomorrah. Lot selected by sight. Abraham selected by faith.

Abraham also demonstrated his natural weakness in that when God promised Abraham he would give him a son, Abraham believed God but allowed his wife, Sarah, to persuade him that God needed some help. Abraham had waited a long time for God to give him a son, so Sarah convinced him that he could have a son with Hagar, Sarah's servant.

God never needs our help; he only needs our faith. God kept his promise to Abraham and did give him a son. Abraham now had two sons, but only Isaac, the son of Sarah, was the son of promise. Isaac would become the patriarch of Israel.

Abraham also demonstrated tremendous faith when he was willing to sacrifice his son Isaac. It must have taken unwavering trust and faith for him to trust God to the point to be willing to step outside his comfort zone and be willing to sacrifice his only son. Abraham's faith led him to believe that God is faithful and just and will always provide a way out. God's way out provided for Abraham was a ram caught in the bushes.

God had a ram for Abraham.

How Do We Apply the Story of Abraham?

Abraham was an ordinary person with all the frailties and weaknesses of most, and had a strong faith in God. God was able to use Abraham because of his faith. God will sometimes test our faith before he can use us. Most of the biblical heroes went through tremendous testing and, in many cases, hardships before God used them. Noah preached about a storm for forty years. John the Baptist was beheaded. Most of the disciples were martyred. Even the apostle Paul was beheaded.

Like most, Abraham was called upon to step outside his comfort zone, to leave his home and go to a foreign land, but the most difficult test of faith was when God commanded Abraham to kill his own son. Because of his faith, God provided a ram for him.

God sometimes call on us to step outside our comfort zone, to even move away from our loved ones and go to a place he has commanded. God may sometimes command us to give up the person or thing we love the most, but just as God provided a ram for Abraham, God will always provide something better than what God asked you to give up.

God allowed Satan to take away everything that Job owned—Job's cattle, Job's home, Job's wealth, Job's family, and even Job's health—but Job continued to trust God. God always blesses those who trust him and are faithful. Job was blessed by God because of his trust and faith. God restored a double portion of what Job formerly had (Job 42:10–17).

So when you see a friend or family member that appears to be going through trials and about to give up or make the mistake that Abraham and Sarah did by doing something their way rather than the way God commanded, tell them that "God always blesses what he commands us to do but not necessarily what we choose to do" (Dr. Larry Mercer). Tell them to step out in faith outside their comfort zone, to trust God and do what God commanded and receive the blessing God has for them because

"God has a ram for you."

CHAPTER 4

God Calls Moses

"I Have a Rod for You"

The beginning of the life of Moses is recorded in the book of Exodus in the Holy Bible. At the time of Moses's birth, the Egyptians who had enslaved the Israelites were becoming fearful of the way the Israelites were increasing in population. The Egyptian Pharaoh was worried that the increasing population of the Israelites would make them able to ally with some of the Egyptian's enemies and overthrow them.

The Egyptian Pharaoh therefore issued an order that all newborn male babies were to be put to death. Moses's Hebrew mother, Jochebed, hid her son Moses in a basket and placed him in the Nile River to keep the Egyptians from finding and killing him.

Moses was later found floating in the Nile River by Pharaoh's daughter. She adopted Moses and raised him as her son in the royal family. Moses possessed all the comforts of royalty, but was called to step outside his comfort zone when he witnessed a Hebrew slave being mistreated by an Egyptian slave master.

Moses's story begins in the book of Exodus, but Moses is an extension of the promise made by God to Abraham that God through Abraham would create a great nation. Moses was chosen by God to be the deliverer of that nation to set the captives free.

Moses did not fit any of the characteristics most would consider to be the leader of a nation. Moses's legitimacy was even challenged by his own family. His sister Miriam and his brother Aaron criticized him for marrying a foreigner, Zipporah, a Midianite. Moses also had a speech impediment. He appeared not to possess any of the qualities of a leader and was often challenged by his followers. The apostle Paul would later write in Romans 8:31, "If God is for us, then who can be against us."

Romans 8:31 is demonstrated throughout the life of Moses. Whenever Moses was attacked whether by his enemies or his own family, God was with Moses and provided for him. When Moses questioned his own leadership ability by saying he could not approach Pharaoh because of his speech impediment, God provided Aaron. When Pharaoh would not listen to Moses, God allowed Moses to use the rod he had provided him with. When Moses and the Israelites were faced with the Red Sea, God again allowed Moses to use the rod he had provided him with. Before Moses's encounter with God, he only had a stick in his hands; with God, Moses now had the rod of God in his hands.

How Do We Apply the Story of Moses?

The story of Moses again demonstrates how God can use ordinary and insignificant people with what we may consider having human weaknesses and disabilities to perform extraordinary task with an ordinary piece of material. The story of Moses demonstrates (Rom. 8:31) even if your family turns against you, they will not prevail if God be for you.

The story of Moses demonstrates that we may have to confront enemies or, as Moses, the Red Seas of life, but just as God provided a rod for Moses, He will provide for you. God has gifted each one of his children with a very special talent to use to confront the Pharaohs of life or the Red Seas of life. So when you are confronted with your enemies or the Red Seas of life and there appears to be no way out, God wants you to step outside your comfort zone on faith because

"God has a rod for you."

CHAPTER 5

God Calls David

God Has a Stone for You

At the time of David's call by the Lord, Israel, God's chosen people, were bickering because they wanted to be like other nations. They wanted to be ruled by a king. God had delivered the children of Israel out of bondage. The children of Israel had been led by Moses, then by Joshua. The Lord had provided for them, but they still wanted a king.

Saul became the first king of Israel. Choosing Saul as king, the children of Israel were rejecting the Lord as their king. "For they have rejected me from being king over them" (1 Sam. 8:6–7). Samuel spoke on behalf of the Lord, warning them regarding requesting a king.

Saul began as a good king but soon became caught up in Saul and strayed away from God. Saul did not follow the commandments of God.

He was the children of Israel's choice for king, not the Lord's. The Lord would reject Saul as king but would choose a king and more would be written about the king God chose than any other person in the Bible.

God sent Samuel to the house of Jesse to select the next king of Israel. Samuel would have chosen one of Jesse's other sons, but God had chosen the one least likely to have been chosen by man. Samuel, like most, was looking at the physical status, not the heart. God was looking at the heart.

When Samuel arrived at Jesse's house to select the next king of Israel, Jesse marched seven of his sons in front of Samuel, starting with Elijah, and Samuel thought for sure this would be God's choice, but God rejected him as well as the other six sons of Jesse.

Samuel then asked, "Is there any other sons?" and Jesse said, "Only the youngest who is tending sheep." God chose David and stated that man looks at the outward appearance, but God looks at the heart. David was chosen by God to be the next king of Israel.

David had only been a shepherd boy caring for sheep. A sheepherder was considered a very menial, insignificant job. David had spent many lonely days and nights alone with his father's sheep. But this was God's training ground for his chosen king. God knew David's heart and instructed Samuel not to judge the new king by height or vision (1 Sam. 17).

Saul was still the children of Israel's chosen king, but David was God's chosen king. Israel had been in battle with the Philistines and all Israel's army was afraid of one of the Philistines' champion, Goliath. Goliath was a giant among men that made even King Saul fearful.

King Saul and the Israel Army all joked when the shepherd boy David said he would take on the giant with only a sling and a few stones. Goliath, the giant, also made jokes of David and his stones. What Goliath, King Saul, and the Israel Army found out on that day was the stones that David had were stones of God.

David was able to defeat Goliath with just a stone because God had prepared him when he was just a shepherd boy. He had used a stone before to kill a loin and a bear when they tried to attack his father's sheep. David went on to become the greatest king of Israel.

How Do We Apply the Story of David?

There are so many examples of how we can use the illustration of the life of David in our lives. I often use the example of David in explaining to my children when they complain about being mistreated or overlooked for a position or promotion, as well as other situations in my life where I have personally used the example of David's life to make decisions.

David was first overlooked when Samuel came to anoint a king. Samuel, like most of us, was looking at outward appearance. God instructed Samuel not to consider height or outward appearance for man because God looks at the heart. 1 Sam 16;7.

Far too often in life we make the mistake of judging people by their height or outward appearance. We sometimes have a tendency to judge people's spirituality by their outward appearances. The ones that appear to be so spiritual outwardly during church service that will stand, wave their hands, and scream are all outward expressions that may have nothing to do with spirituality. God sees the heart and, unlike man, judges our hearts and not our outward expressions.

David was the youngest of Jesse's sons and the least likely to have been selected to be king. But God's thoughts are not our thoughts (Isa. 55:8–9). God had prepared David as a shepherd boy to someday be king, which is another illustration of Colossians 3:23–24: "Whatever you do, work at it with all your heart, as working for the Lord, not for human masters."

David had spent many days doing the lowly job of caring for his father's sheep. He protected the sheep when a bear attempted to harm them. David protected them when a lion attempted to harm them. He didn't realize that in learning to be a good shepherd in the lowly job of caring for sheep, God was preparing him for a lofty job of being a good king over God's people. What lowly job are you doing that God may be preparing you for some lofty job?

David was constantly in danger and on the run from King Saul, who made numerous attempts to kill him. The people of Israel wanted David to be their king, but David understood God had a special time for him to be king. David is most noted in the Bible for killing the giant Goliath with a stone. So when you see a friend or family member facing the giants of life, tell them, "God wants you to step outside your comfort zone in faith."

Many people fail to step outside their comfort zone to respond and to perform their godly call because of critics and what discouraging people say. I am sure many discouraged David by saying, "The giant is too big, you are too small. You have not been to giant-killing school." Sometimes it can be one's closest associates or family that can be one's biggest critics. David's own brothers criticized and discouraged him and told him to go back home and take care of their father's sheep, but David understood that "if God is for you who can be against you?" (Rom. 8:31). God did not just provide a stone for David; God guided that stone like a guided missile to the right spot.

So when the giants of life appear and God has called upon you to step outside your comfort zone to take on these giants, don't stand around wondering what your critics are saying. Remember,

"God has a stone for you."

CHAPTER 6

God Calls Jonah

God Has a Fish for You

The book of Jonah is one of the shortest books in the Bible but is one that contains more theology than probably any other book in the Bible. The book of Jonah illustrates God's sovereignty over nature more than any other book in the Bible.

God commands the wind, and the wind obeys and creates a great storm. God commands a fish, and the fish obeys and swallows up Jonah. God calls the wind again, and again the wind obeys and ceases to blow. God calls the fish again, and again the fish obeys and vomits up its dinner, Jonah. God calls a tree, and the tree obeys and grows up to provide shade for Jonah. God calls a worm, and the worm obeys and causes the tree to wither. God calls the tree again, and again the tree obeys and returns to provide shade for Jonah. God calls man, and man disobeys.

Some English translations hold that Jonah was swallowed up by a whale, but the original Hebrew text actually uses the phrase dag gadol, which means "great fish," but whether it was a great fish or a whale, the fact remains: the sea creature obeyed God.

The prophet Jonah prophesies during the reign of Jeroboam II (786–746 BC) in the northern kingdom of Israel. The word of the Lord came to Jonah, the son of Amittqi, saying, "Arise and go to Nineveh that great city, and cry against it; for their wickedness is come up before me."

Nineveh was the capital city of Assyria with about one-half million people. It was the entertaining city of its day, like today's Las Vegas. Jonah is called by God to go to Nineveh, a city that is so sinful, until God calls Jonah to step outside his comfort zone and go preach repentance. Jonah disobeys God, boards a ship, and travels in the opposite direction toward Tarshish.

Jonah didn't just disobey God; he went in the opposite direction of where God had ordered him to go. Because of Jonah's disobedience, God calls the wind to stir up a storm that is about to destroy the ship that Jonah is on. Jonah understands God and knows the storm is formed because of his disobedience to God's call. He therefore tells the ship's crew why the storm formed and to throw him overboard to stop the storm.

God then calls a great fish that sees Jonah in the water as his dinner. God sees the great fish as Jonah's salvation. The fish swallows up Jonah. Jonah is in the belly of the great fish for three days. While in the belly of the great fish, he repents and prays to God.

God hears Jonah's prayer from the belly of the great fish and calls the fish to travel to shore and to vomit up Jonah on dry land. Jonah then obeys God's call and goes to Nineveh and preaches repentance to the people, and the people respond and are saved.

The book also illustrates how it is impossible to run from God. Jonah's disobedience only created problems for him as well as those around him. But God also demonstrated his faithfulness, mercy, and forgiveness by giving him a second chance. When Jonah obeyed God's call and stepped outside his comfort zone to obey the call of God, the king and a whole nation were saved.

How Do We Apply the Story of Jonah?

The book of Jonah is a great illustration of God's sovereignty over nature, but not just nature but all of creation. The book also demonstrates how it is impossible to run from the call of God. It demonstrates how God is a God of mercy and will give a second chance to those who will repent and obey his call. The book of Jonah also teaches us that even though we may appear to be swallowed up by unthinkable problems, God will sometimes use what we see as a problem to be our salvation. The fish saw Jonah as dinner; Jonah saw the fish as his final hopeless disaster. God saw and used the fish as Jonah's salvation and an opportunity to demonstrate his glory and power by commanding the wind and the sea, "Hush! Be still!"

We can also see many other examples throughout the Bible and in many personal testimonies where God has demonstrated his sovereignty over all of creation. Just as God demonstrated his sovereignty over nature in the book of Jonah, God also demonstrated his sovereignty over all of creation by commanding sickness in the book of Luke to "hush, be still," when he healed the woman with an issue of blood (Luke 8:43–48). God, also in the book of John, demonstrated his power and sovereignty even over death by telling death to "hush, be still" when he raised Lazarus from the dead (John 11:38–44).

So when the problems and storms of life appear to engulf you, when it appears you are faced with your last hopeless disaster, remember, God wants you to step outside your comfort zone in faith because God may want to use your hopeless disaster, your messed-up life, your sickness, even death to demonstrate his sovereignty, glory, and power through you. God only has to speak the words "Hush! Be still."

The songwriter stated, "There is no secret what God can do; what he has done for others, he'll do for you, with arms wide open, he is calling you, what he has done for others, he'll do for you." God is and has always been in control of his universe. There is nothing that happens without God commanding it or allowing it.

God allowed Jonah to experience some hardships because of his disobedience. God was faithful and commanded the same fish that Jonah saw as his disaster to become his salvation. God can turn what we see as a disaster into our salvation. God always has the last call.

Always remember!

"God has a fish for you."

CHAPTER 7

God Calls His Disciples

God Has a Mission for You

One of the most significant and historical calls God has ever made for a person to step outside their comfort zone to perform a mission for God was the calling of the twelve disciples. Most of the men God called to be his disciples were just everyday, ordinary men that were called on to perform extraordinary things.

According to the Gospel of Mark (1:16), as he walked by the Sea of Galilee, he saw Simon and Andrew his brother casting their nets into the sea; for they were fishers. And Jesus said, "Come ye after me and I will make you fishers of men." Mark records they straightway forsook their nets and followed Jesus. Jesus also called his brothers James and John, who were on their father Zebedee's ship. When they received the call, they immediately dropped what they were doing and left their father to follow Jesus.

The calling of the disciples demonstrates the great sacrifice one may have to make in order to accept and follow the call of God. Simon and Andrew stepped outside their comfort zone and left their jobs and their property. James and John stepped outside their comfort zone and left their jobs and father to follow Jesus. While one may be required to make a great sacrifice to follow Jesus, God promised the reward cannot be compared to the sacrifice.

Jesus continued to minister and called disciples until there were twelve. These twelve followed Jesus and witnessed many miracles and wonders performed by him. Following Jesus appeared to be easy because Jesus was turning water into wine, giving sight to the blind, feeding five thousand with only two fish and five loaves of bread, and raising the dead. Who wouldn't want to follow a person that could do all that? But Jesus did not just come to be a welfare God or a healer of all illnesses. God has the power to just speak the word and there would be no more illness, hunger, or death; but that was not Jesus's reason for appearing. Jesus appeared to correct the mistake made by Adam. In the Garden of Eden, Adam had fallen for a foul ball thrown by Satan. On the cross, Jesus would hit a home run with the same foul ball thrown by Satan.

Jesus understood a lot of people were following him for the wrong reasons. In the Gospel of John (6:26), Jesus tells the people that followed him after the feeding of the five thousand, "Verily, verily, I say unto you, ye seek me, not because ye saw the miracles, but because ye did eat of the loaves and were filled." Jesus recognized many of his followers were not following him because of his message but were following him for what they could get and for what they had seen him provide in the material things. Jesus came to provide a gift much more valuable than the material things many seek even today.

This is one of the major problems with many churches and ministries today. Far too many people go into the ministry not because of the message of Jesus but for what they can get. Many ministries today look and function more like a business than a ministry. Many ministries today are becoming earthly wealthy while becoming heavenly bankrupt. Far too many people who cannot achieve wealth and recognition in the traditional professions turn to the ministry. One has referred to this as pimping Jesus.

Far too many people in ministries today are living in total contradiction to how Jesus's and his disciples' ministries were. As stated earlier, the disciples gave up everything in order to follow Jesus. Today many ministers want to get everything they can in order to follow Jesus.

Peter even apparently left his wife. Matthew 8:14 mentions Peter's mother-in-law. Matthew 8 also mentions the healing of Peter's mother-in-law.

Jesus stated, "The foxes have holes, the birds of the air have nests but the Son of man hath no place to lay his head" (Matt. 8:20). Jesus understood people were following him for what he could provide them temporarily and earthly, but what Jesus had come to provide for them was heavenly and eternal. Just as in Jesus's time, many are in the ministry today for the temporary earthly benefit rather than for the eternal heavenly reward.

Jesus generally called for his disciples to drop or give up whatever they were doing to follow him. Many had excuses as to why they could not follow him. One had to bury his father; another had to say goodbye to his family, but one in particular Jesus mentioned was the rich young ruler.

"Looking at him, Jesus felt a love for him and said to him, 'Go sell all your possessions and give to the poor, and you will have treasure in heaven; and come and follow me'" (Mark 10:17–27). Jesus offered to this rich young ruler the opportunity to be one of his disciples, but because the rich young ruler loved possessions, he forfeited the opportunity. How many of us will miss the opportunity because of our love for earthly possessions?

The disciple Peter is mentioned more in the Bible than any other disciple of Jesus. Peter gets a bad name because he is most remembered for denying Jesus. But the Scripture tells far greater things about Peter than his denial of Jesus. Jesus understood the weakness of Peter just as he understands our weaknesses. Peter's weaknesses did not disqualify him, nor do our weaknesses disqualify us from being used by God.

Peter was the very first disciple Jesus called. When God chose to reveal his deity, he chose Peter, for Peter confessed, "You are the Christ the Son of the living God" (Matt. 16:16). God had not revealed his deity to the other disciples. Peter was also the only disciple to step outside his comfort zone and walk on water (Matt. 14:29). He attempted to defend Jesus by cutting off the ear of one of the soldiers that was trying to arrest Jesus (John 18:10).

The Scripture does state Peter denied Jesus three times after Jesus's capture, but what is rarely questioned is where were the other disciples.

They were all present when Jesus was captured, but the Scripture only records Peter following Jesus. Peter is the only disciple that is mentioned after Jesus's capture.

After the resurrection of Jesus, Peter becomes the rock, the pillow of the first church. Peter clearly becomes the leader and a bold, outspoken person for Jesus. His boldness and outspokenness cause him to be crucified. When Peter is faced with being crucified, he declares he is not worthy enough to be crucified like Jesus but should be crucified upside down.

How Do We Apply the Call of the Disciples?

When Jesus called his disciples, he chose ordinary men but men that were willing to step outside their comfort zone and give up everything to follow him. We have so many so-called religious leaders today that are willing to follow Jesus but not willing to give up everything. In many cases, it is just the opposite. They are willing to follow Jesus only if it means a gain for them. Sometimes that gain may be property, and sometimes that gain may be the praise and recognition from others.

Matthew 6:1–34 warns us about leaders who practice righteousness to receive praise and recognition from others. The Bible refers to these as hypocrites that seek praise by publicly giving or openly and publicly praying to be seen by others rather than to be heard by God. The Bible states they have received their reward.

The calling of the disciples demonstrates how God uses ordinary people who are willing to step outside their comfort zone to do extraordinary things. For those that are willing to answer the call, God has a crown for you.

The disciples gave up everything to follow Jesus. They were persecuted, imprisoned, beaten, and even martyred for their following of Jesus. Sometimes we may feel like we have sacrificed, been persecuted for our faith, but just as Paul stated in Romans 8:18, "I consider that our present suffering is not worth comparing with the glory that will be revealed in us."

"Henceforth there is laid up for me a crown of righteousness, which the Lord, the righteous judge, shall give me at that day; and not to me only but unto all them also that love his appearing" (2 Tim. 4:8).

When you can encourage a friend who feels persecuted for following the Word of God, remember, your persecution is not worth comparing to God's reward for you. "After all we brought nothing into this world, and we can take nothing out of it" (1 Tim. 6:7). Why would anyone try to hold on to something they can't keep and give up what they can't lose? We can't keep any property acquired on earth; we can't lose our crown. Our mission in life should always be willing to step outside our comfort zone for the task in which God has called us to perform. We will be welcomed with the words "Well done, good and faithful servant" (Matt. 25:23).

"God has a 'Well done, good and faithful servant' for you."

CHAPTER 8

God Calls the Apostle Paul

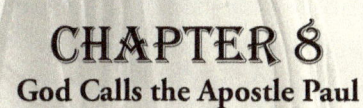

God Has a Crown for You

The apostle Paul is the most important figure in the Bible next to Jesus. The apostle Paul is the perfect example of how God is able to use anyone who is willing to step outside their comfort zone to answer God's call. Paul, also known by his Jewish name Saul, had been a persecutor of God's church and was on his way to Damascus to persecute Christians when he received his call from God.

After Paul's conversion, he became the main character in the New Testament of the Bible. During his life Paul founded several churches in Asia Minor and Europe. Paul is also attributed with having written most of the books of the New Testament. Thirteen of the twenty-seven books of the New Testament are generally considered to have been written by Paul. Most Christian churches today follow and practice the teachings of Paul. Paul's Epistles are by far the most used books in training pastors for most Christian churches even today.

Paul is also noted for making several missionary trips to evangelize in several countries. He wrote the saints in Rome from Corinth during his third missionary trip because he had a great desire to visit Rome to evangelize the Christians there. Paul had many followers but also had many that did not agree with him and his ministry.

The apostle Paul's life wasn't just about writing books, going on missionary trips, and founding churches. Paul experienced and endured many trials and much suffering in the name of the Gospel. Paul was first blinded on his way from Jerusalem to Damascus but was able to regain his sight after obeying God. This was only the beginning of the trials and suffering he would endure in the name of the Gospel.

Paul was a prisoner several times, beaten, and shipwrecked. As Paul and others were crossing the Adriatic Sea at about midnight, the sailors realized the ship was in trouble and let down the lifeboats. They had decided to abandon the ship and try to escape their disaster by using the lifeboats, but Paul told them the only way to survive was to stay with the ship.

As morning came, they could see land and knew the ship was going to be destroyed once it hit land. The sailors decided to kill all the prisoners including Paul to keep them from escaping, but the centurion ordered all prisoners who could swim be allowed to try to swim to shore and the ones that could not be allowed to float on pieces of planks from the broken ship. Paul was able to float to safety on a plank from the wrecked ship.

After reaching shore and supposedly safety, the survivors were gathering wood to build a fire.

As Paul picked up a piece of wood, a viper under the wood bit Paul and was clinging to his hand. Paul put the snake in the fire and appeared not to be seriously injured even though the others thought the bite from the viper should have killed him.

Paul was beaten and imprisoned many times in the name of the Gospel. He would later be charged with a capital offense for taking Greeks into the temple, which was considered defiling the temple. Greeks were not allowed to enter the temple.

Paul would eventually be tried, convicted, and beheaded with a sword near Rome for the work he was doing to reach out and evangelize the Gentiles. It has been said that Paul poured out his life like a drink offering to the Lord. Before his death, he courageously stated, "For me to live is Christ; to die is to gain" (Phil. 1:21).

Paul's life was totally changed after he received his call to the ministry. He was a proud, respected Roman Citizen who had authority from the high priest to imprison and punish believers before he received his call. Paul even participated in the stoning of Stephen. After accepting his call, Paul suffered and became an outcast and a prisoner of Rome and would eventually be executed. But through it all and in the end, Paul stated, "I consider that our present sufferings are not comparable to the glory that will be revealed to us" (Rom. 8:18).

Paul always stayed focused and understood his purpose for being created and being called by God to step outside his comfort zone. "Brothers, I do not consider that I have made it on my own. But one thing I do; forget what lies behind and straining forward to what lies ahead, I press on forward toward the goal for the prize of the upward call of God in Christ Jesus" (Phil. 3:13–14).

How Do We Apply the Life of the Apostle Paul?

There are so many lessons we can learn and use from the life of the apostle Paul after his encounter on his way to Damascus. One of the best lessons Paul taught us was on being content with whatever hand life has dealt us. Paul's life was spent in constant danger from both his own countrymen as well as his opposition. Paul had a thorn in his flesh, he spent a considerable amount of time in prison, he was beaten, shipwrecked, bitten by a deadly viper, but Paul wrote, "I have learned the secret of being content in any and every situation" (Phil. 4:12).

One of the major problems in society today is not being content and satisfied with where God has placed you. Most crimes are caused by one wanting something that belongs to someone else. Most breakups of families are because of not being content and satisfied with the spouse one has. Most job dissatisfactions and frustrations come from not being content and satisfied with the job God has provided.

Throughout Paul's life after his conversion, he stayed focused on what was most important, and that was not the little temporary pains and problems of life but the bigger prize, "his crown." "Henceforth there is laid up for me a crown" (2 Tim. 4:8).

Tell your family and friends when you see them complaining about their jobs, their spouse, their finances, their health that these are only temporary problems and they should be content and satisfied with where God has placed them. Tell them God has a crown laid up for them so long as they keep the faith.

"God has a crown for you."

CHAPTER 9

God Calls Harriet Tubman

God Has a Railroad for You

Harriet Tubman was born in 1820 a slave. Tubman was able to escape from slavery and could have lived as a free woman, but she had a calling. Tubman stepped outside her comfort zone at least thirteen times, risking her own freedom returning to help rescue some seventy enslaved people using what became known as the Underground Railroad.

Tubman had established a relationship with a number of White sympathizers who were opposed to slavery that would allow Tubman and her runaway slaves to hide in barns, cellars, or wherever they could while they were making their way to freedom. This was very dangerous for Tubman as well as for those who aided her. But they were willing to step outside their comfort zone to do a godly deed. When we read about all the cruelties of slavery, we must also read and understand that there were godly Whites who were willing to risk their lives and step outside their comfort zone to help.

Tubman is best known for her work with the Underground Railroad freeing slaves, but she later assisted John Brown in recruiting men for his raid on Harpers Ferry. She also served her country during the Civil War as an army scout and a spy.

How Do We Apply the Harriet Tubman Story?

Harriet Tubman's life demonstrates that we should have a responsibility and calling to step outside our comfort zone when God has given us a talent or freedom, as in Harriet Tubman's case, to use that talent or freedom to aid and help others when we have been helped or freed. God blesses us so that we likewise can bless others. We may have not been set free from physical slavery, but we may have been set free from financial slavery. We should use our financial freedom and knowledge to help someone else who is in financial slavery. It may be we can use our freedom from drug addiction to help someone else to become drug-free. Whatever God has blessed us with and helped us to be free from, we have a responsibility to use that freedom to help others.

CHAPTER 10
God Calls Rosa Parks

God Has a Better Seat for You

In 1955 Rosa Parks was a typical African American that understood the times and understood how society expected her to follow the norms of the times. But on December 1, 1955, Rosa Parks would be called upon to step outside her comfort zone. Her decision to answer the call to step outside her comfort zone came at a high price and personal sacrifice to her and her family, as it does many times when God calls us to step outside our comfort zone. Little did Rosa Park know that her decision would start a movement that would change a whole nation. God's plan may cause us to make a sacrifice and be uncomfortable, but God's reward for obedience can never be compared to our little discomfort.

In 1955 most southern cities in the United States had their segregation laws. These laws treated certain citizens (African Americans) as second-class citizens. African Americans could not attend the best schools, could not be employed at the best jobs, could not eat at most restaurants, and could not use the public libraries. But most shamefully, they could not attend church at some churches—God's church.

On December 1, 1955, Rosa Parks had worked hard all day, boarded a Montgomery, Alabama, bus for a peaceful ride home. After boarding the bus, she proceeded, as was the law to the colored section of the bus. The front seats were reserved for White-only passengers. When the White-only section became full, the bus driver came to the Colored section and told Mrs. Parks she would have to give up her seat for a White passenger. A bus driver could change the seating arrangement at will. Mrs. Parks was sitting in the Colored section of the bus, but when the White-only section filled up, the bus driver changed the seating arrangement to make more room for a White passenger by requiring Mrs. Parks to give up her seat.

Mrs. Parks, who would later say she was tired from her long day at work and tired from the many years of mistreatment of African Americans, flatly refused to do so. She was arrested and charged with civil disobedience. Her arrest outraged the local African American community and brought attention nationwide to show just how unfair and unjust the segregated systems were.

The Montgomery, Alabama, Municipal Bus System was 70 percent African American. So the leadership of the African American community decided to boycott the bus system. For almost a year African Americans refused to ride the buses. The bus system could not survive very long with 70 percent of the customary passengers no longer riding the bus. The bus company suffered financially and could no longer exist.

Finally, on June 5, 1956, a Montgomery federal court ruled that any law requiring racially segregated seating on buses violated the Fourteenth Amendment to the United States Constitution. The boycott had been a success but at a cost to Mrs. Parks and her family. Mrs. Parks was arrested and went to jail. She was fired from her job, and so was her husband. The African Americans that participated in the boycott had to endure for over a year struggling to get transportation to and from places they normally caught the bus.

Rosa Park died on October 5, 2005, a national heroine with the United States Senate passing a resolution to honor Parks by allowing her body to lie in honor in the US Capitol Rotunda. Parks's decision to step outside her comfort zone also brought about the election of Dr. Martin

L. King to lead the boycott. Dr. King would later be recognized as one of America's greatest leader.

History would be unfair and incomplete if it did not mention the name of a fifteen-year-old young African American girl named Claudette Colvin, who at the young age of fifteen defied the same segregated laws that made Rosa Parks a part of American history. Claudette had been put off a bus in Montgomery, Alabama, nine months before Rosa Parks and for the same reasons as Rosa Parks.

How Do We Apply the Story of Rosa Parks?

The problems of life will sometimes seem too difficult to bear. Sometimes we may become dismayed and want to give up. Sometimes we may feel too tired to carry on. The story of Rosa Parks lets us know, God is always in control and God knows just how much we can bear, and God will always provide a seat for us.

"God has a seat for you."

CHAPTER 11

God Calls Dr. Martin L. King Jr.

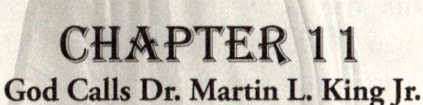

God Has a Dream for You

Martin L. King Jr., the son of a prominent Baptist minister, was born in Atlanta, Georgia, in 1929. Dr. King received his undergraduate degree from Morehouse University in Atlanta and his doctorate degree in theology from Boston University. He would later be influenced by Mohandas Gandhi, an Indian attorney, on nonviolence protest. Dr. King would become one of America's greatest orators and became famous for his "I Have a Dream" speech in Washington, DC, in 1963.

In 1955 the Montgomery bus boycott created national attention on just how horrible Blacks were discriminated against in many of the Southern states under the Jim Crow laws. In Montgomery, Black citizens were required to enter the front of the bus to pay the same fare as the White passengers but would then be required to exit the front of the bus and enter the back for a seat. When all the seats were filled in the front White section of the bus, White passengers were allowed to go into the Black section of the bus and require a Black person to give up their seat.

This boycott caught the attention of Dr. Martin L. King Jr. Dr. King would be later called upon to step outside his comfort zone as a prominent minister and pastor to take on the unjust Jim Crow laws and practices of the South. Dr. King became the leader of the Montgomery Bus Boycott Movement. This would propel Dr. King into the national and international spotlight.

Dr. King became nationally and internationally known, but at a great sacrifice. In 1956 Dr. King's house was bombed. He was arrested many times for his participation including being convicted and ordered to serve 386 days in jail. The movement created national attention, which led to a federal court ruling, Browder v. Gayle, that held the Montgomery and other Southern state laws on segregated buses were unconstitutional. The decision was later upheld by the US Supreme Court.

Dr. Martin L. King is most noted for his Montgomery Boycott, "I Have a Dream" speech in Washington, DC, and being the youngest recipient of the Nobel Peace Prize, but his greatest accomplishment was his influence in getting the ratification of the Twenty-Fourth Amendment, which abolished the poll tax and the Civil Rights Act of 1964, which prohibited racial discrimination in employment, education, and outlawed racial segregation in public facilities.

Voting is one of the most powerful tools and rights American citizens have. This is one of the reasons the Jim Crow laws were designed to keep certain citizens from being able to vote. They knew there was power in the right to vote. There were a lot of schemes to prevent certain citizens from exercising their right to vote. The requirements to pay poll taxes and to pass literacy tests for certain citizens were just a few.

This was such a great accomplishment for those that understand the power of the vote and the sacrifices so many people made to ensure each person has the right to vote. Dr. King, Medgar Evers, my dad, and so many others paid the supreme sacrifice for citizens to have the right to vote. This is one of the reasons I get so upset when people won't even take just a few minutes to exercise their right to vote or in some cases sell their vote so cheaply by voting for the wrong person because they have not educated themselves on the person's qualifications, experience, or what they really stand for.

I am thankful I had the privilege and honor of meeting Dr. King twice during my lifetime. I first met him when I was a junior high school student. He came to Mississippi to help lead a march with my dad, who was president of a local branch of the NAACP, along with other civil rights leaders.

My dad was deeply involved in the civil rights movement, which was very dangerous to be in Mississippi at the time. My dad tried to keep his family safe and would not allow me to get involved with the movement. My cousin, who by the way was also named Martin Luther Hays, and I had been told not to go near the demonstration because it would be too dangerous, but we slipped to it anyway.

My cousin Martin Luther came and picked me up on his new motorcycle, and we went to meet Dr. King at the head of the march. We left before the march started and was headed home down an old deserted country dirt road when we discovered we had been followed by a police officer.

When the police officer discovered we were aware of him following us, he pulled us over. We thought we were goners and probably would have been because he tried to set us up by making it appear to be easy for us to try to escape by leaving us on the side of the road for almost an hour while he pretended to be investigating something about a quarter of a mile away.

We did not fall for the bait but remained still on the side of the road in the hot sun until he came back. I can only explain, with all the hatred and anger that existed at the time, why we are alive today except for the grace of God.

I met Dr. King the second time after I had left home to attend college in Dallas, Texas. After arriving in Dallas, Texas, I felt I could get involved in the civil rights movement without endangering my family like it would have had I gotten involved in Mississippi.

In Dallas, I had no family to worry about; it was just me. I was excited to be able to get involved in the movement without fear of what could happen to my family. I first joined the NAACP. The NAACP did not appear to me to be doing very much in Dallas except having a few parties and glorifying some of its members. I did not see very much the NAACP was doing for the cause. I felt so disappointed, so I joined a more radical group, Student Nonviolent Coordinating Committee.

I had grown up being a follower of Medgar Evers, Dr. King, and my dad. These leaders took a more nonviolent approach to issues. There were a lot of students at my school from the North that were followers of leaders that advocated a different approach like Malcolm X, Stokely Carmichael, and Ralph Brown.

I joined up with this group because I thought they had a more direct approach and was getting some attention and some things done. Then in 1968, George Wallace, the segregationist governor of Alabama and presidential candidate, was going to speak in Dallas. We were told that several hundred would gather to protest Mr. Wallace. When we arrived, there were only eight of us. I wanted to call it off, but our self-serving leader saw the cameras and the opportunity to be in the spotlight and refused.

Our leader yelled insults at Mr. Wallace, which interrupted his speech until all the attention and cameras were on us. Mr. Wallace responded by yelling insults at us and encouraging the angry crowd of supporters to throw us out of the prestigious Statler Hilton Hotel, where the event was being held. The angry crowd, now mob, responded and began to mob us. I prayed to the Lord to deliver us and I would never be involved with this group again.

A reporter from the New York Times who was covering the speech approached some Dallas police officers who were just standing by watching us being mobbed and insisted they come to our aid. The police officers finally made a barricade around us to block the angry mob from getting to us, and then one of the Dallas police officers told us to get our Black asses out of Dallas. I never participated with that radical group again.

I still however had the desire to be involved in the civil rights movement. Then later that year, I had my second chance to meet Dr. King. My new hometown, Dallas, Texas, had been quiet and not involved very much in the civil rights movement like most Southern cities. While Dallas, Texas, was just as segregated as most Southern cities, very little was being done. There were very few Black leaders except for the Black preachers who seemed to not want to rock the boat.

I had heard that Dr. Martin L. King Jr. had been invited to speak and lead a peaceful march in South Dallas, the segregated Black part of Dallas. It became really clear; Dallas was not ready for change. The majority of the White citizens didn't want Dr. King in Dallas, so they got their Black ministers who appeared to be the only leadership to join in denouncing Dr. King's visit. The pastor of the largest White church in Dallas, First Baptist, preached and practiced segregation.

Rev. Peter Johnson, a young African American minister, friend, and coworker of Dr. King, also worked with the Southern Christian Leadership Conference, had invited Dr. King to Dallas. It now appeared the Black ministers and the few Black leaders of Dallas had joined with the White citizens to let Dr. King know he was not welcome in Dallas. He was being labeled as an outsider, instigator, and troublemaker that Dallas didn't want.

Rev. Johnson was able to recruit enough young people, mostly students, to meet with Dr. King and to march peacefully in South Dallas. Most of the Black ministers and Black leaders in Dallas refused to participate. I joined with Rev. Johnson and the other students in the march. This was my second time meeting Dr. King. I did not realize it at the time, but this would be the last because Dr. King would be assassinated later that year in Memphis, Tennessee.

CHAPTER 12

God Calls Rev. Steadman Hays

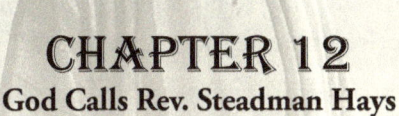

God Has the One for You

(God Created Everything Unique at a Special Time and for a Special Purpose)

The Bible records the many people God called upon and used to carry out his plans, as we have illustrated just a few. Throughout history, and even today, God continues to call people to carry out his plan. God created each person at a special time, unique and different for a unique and special purpose for his plan. Some people understand and accept their call, and some either never understand or will try to run from their calling.

Steadman Hays understood his uniqueness and his special call at a special time in history to carry out a special call from God. He did not run from his calling but was willing to step outside his comfort zone to answer the call of God and to follow the plan God had for his life. Steadman Hays was as unique as everything else God created and demonstrated his uniqueness in the bold way he lived. Unlike most, Steadman Hays almost always chose to take the road less traveled. He, like the philosopher who stated, "If the sky was intended to be the limits, then what in the hell was heaven made for," never saw or accepted limitations placed on him.

We now accept the fact that God created every person just as he created Steadman Hays with a unique and special fingerprint and everything else about him unique and different from every other person he created. Scientists also believe God created every grain of sand unique and different. Scientists have recently discovered that even every leaf on a tree is different with its own unique deoxyribonucleic acid (DNA). Scientists today are discovering that there are probably not two people or two things in this entire universe that is the same.

Scientists today believe that every person is uniquely made and has a different DNA than any other person created. Every part of the human body is different from any other person's body part. Scientists have for many years accepted the fact that no two people have the same fingerprints, handwriting, iris, etc. I was recently told I could be identified by my voice sound, for no two people have the same voice sound.

Scientists say that even every snowflake out of the trillions and trillions that fall across the world each year is different. It appears that the more scientists discover, the more the Bible is proven true. "God knows and named every star in the sky" (Ps. 147:4). "God numbered every hair on your head" (Luke 12:7). Will scientist one day discover that every hair on my head is also different?

We all learned and probably had to recite in school those famous words from the Declaration of Independence: "We hold these truths to be self-evident, that all men are created equal." While these are very beautiful and patriotic words, they are not biblical because there is no place in the Bible or God's Word that says that God created all men equal. God created each person unique and different with different degrees of gifts and talents.

It should therefore follow that if God made everything in the universe different, he probably and most certainly created every man and woman different, with their own and unique DNA and at a unique special time and purpose for being created. It appears the smarter man becomes, the more man validates God's Word. "Behold, I knew you before I formed you in your mother's womb" (Jer. 1:5).

Dr. Larry Mercer, in one of his sermons recently delivered at the Oak Cliff Bible Fellowship Church in Dallas, Texas, stated it best when he said, "God created every person on purpose for a purpose." Dr. Mercer went on to say that many people miss their calling because they sleepwalk through life and never accomplish their divine calling. He further stated that many miss their calling because they fail to realize that "accomplishing God's will is based on a divine invitation and not on human ingenuity."

If God made each person unique and different, it should follow that God made each person for a unique purpose. Each person has a unique purpose in God's plan. "We are God's workmanship, created in Christ Jesus for good works which God prepared beforehand, that we should walk in them" (Eph. 2:10). We can either answer the call of God, follow the plan he has for our life and our creation, or we can try to run as Jonah attempted to do from our Nineveh calling and the world misses out on what God created us to do, or God will accomplish his goal another way.

Many people miss their calling because they fear stepping outside their comfort zone of not being qualified, not being justified, not being significant enough or the fear of being criticized.

Many people would not fear stepping outside their comfort zone if they only understood these simple principles like the one my mom used to tell us: "The only person that is not criticized is the person that does nothing," or God does not call the qualified; he qualifies the ones he calls. God does not call the justified; he justifies the ones he calls. God calls the insignificant to perform significant tasks.

Before Jonah answered the call of God and stepped outside his comfort zone, a whole nation was condemned, but through Jonah's obedience, a whole nation was saved. When Steadman Hays answered the call of God and stepped outside his comfort zone to respond, he set the stage for a better life for his entire family and many people around him.

In order to fully understand why Steadman Hays was created and his special and unique call to step outside his comfort zone at a very special time in history to answer God's call for his life, we must go back in history to discover Steadman Hays's roots. After discovering Steadman Hays's roots, we will show what Steadman Hays's world was like and how God used that situation to inspire him to step outside his comfort zone to try to make the world a better place for his family and his community.

Searching for Our Family Roots
The Walter Hays Family Genealogy

My family recently attempted to trace our family history. We understood our ancestors were brought to America from Africa as slaves. We discovered during our research that during slavery, slaves were not recorded in the Bureau of Census or the records of vital statistics. We were therefore only able to trace our family history back to Antney Hays, born 1827, a slave, died 1898 a free man.

Antney Hays was my grandfather's grandfather. Antney Hays's grave, along with his wife, Caroline, is still located on the banks of Interstate Highway 49 in Simpson County, Mississippi. The date of their birth and deaths are still visible on their marble tombstones.

Two lonely tombstones in the shadow of Interstate Highway 49 in Simpson County, Mississippi

Antney Hays born a slave in 1827 and his wife, Caroline Hays, born a slave in 1842 must have been very special. They were both buried in the all-White cemetery with their slave master's family, and they both appeared to have had very expensive burial sites based on their marble tombstones that still stand today.

A close-up view of their tombstones can be seen on the next page. Both of these tombstones are still erected on the banks of Interstate Highway 49 in Simpson County, Mississippi.

Tombstone of Croline Hays, born1842

The tombstone of Antney Hays, born 1827

Both of these tombstones are still in place along the
banks of Interstate Highway 49 in Simpson County, Mississippi

According to family, Antney Hays and his wife lived in the big house with their slave master and his family. They were therefore treated a little bit better than the field slaves. They took care of the master and his family. Antney Hays also had a skill. He was a leather craftsman. Part of his job was to make shoes for the other slaves and people on the plantations.

Antney Hays and his wife, Caroline, had, according to our research, six children: Washington, born 1860; Sallie, born 1864; Bettie, born 1867; Daniel, born 1872; Glascow, born 1875; and Albert, born 1878. When Antney and his wife died, they were buried in their master's White cemetery. They were the only two Blacks buried there.

One of Antney Hays and Caroline's children was named Washington Hays. Washington Hays married the love of his life, Malinda, who was also a slave on William Hays's plantation. Washington Hays and his wife, Malinda, according to our research and her tombstone, born 1865, had nine children: Ancie, born 1880; James, born 1882; Lula, born 1884; Tomie, born 1886; John, born 1887; Walter (my grandfather), born 1890; Caroline, born 1894; Martha, born 1896; and Hattie, born 1898.

Walter Hays (my grandfather) was born in 1890, and his wife, Annie, was born in 1901. They had nine children: Roosevelt, born 1916; Steadman (my father), born 1918; Walter Jr., born 1920; Aletha, born 1924; William, born 1925; Delma, born 1927; Annie Pearl, born 1928; Martha and Johnnie Neil.

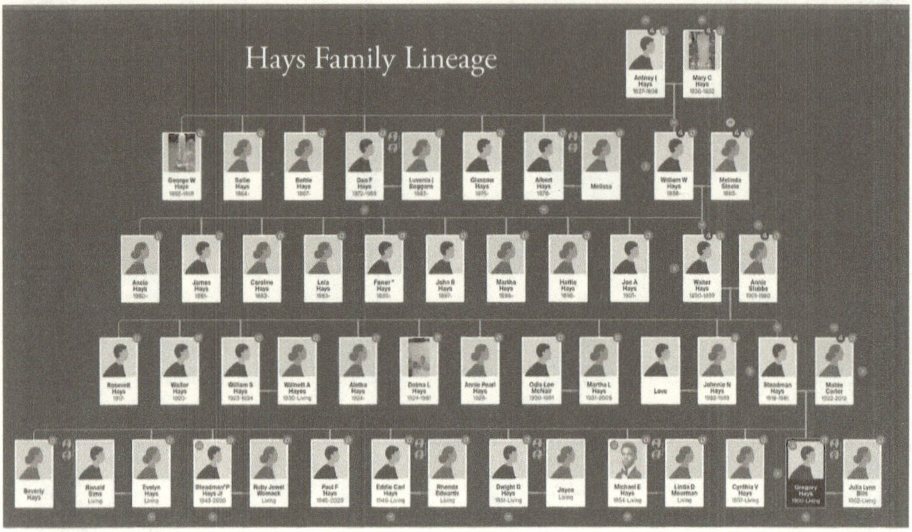

In the 1930s a project was organized to try to interview as many as possible surviving slaves in the state of Mississippi. The Federal Writers, as part of the Works Project Administration, recorded the life stories of many surviving slaves. One of those interviewed was Washington Hays (my grandfather's father). This is Washington Hays's actual unedited interview:

"My grand pappy was a slave in Virgiana but was sole away when pa was a small boy. We don't know who bought him or whar he went as he was took off wid a heap o' others to be sole down de country. Den when my pa was fourteen years old he was sole at a auction to Wane Anderson, a slave trader. He say he was brung down here in a covered wagon. Dey would stop at points an' sell some ob de slaves but my pa was held 'till he got to Mississippi whar he was sole to my ole Marse William Hayes.

"My grand mammy was named Caroline an' she was sole to traders from Virgiana an' brung down to Mississippi. She never did see her people no more. She met grand pappy down here an' dey got married. It happened dey was on de same plantation. Yo' see Marse Billy owned three purty good size plantations wid several families o' slaves on each one. He had over-seers to look after 'em an' he rode a fine purty ho'se from one to de other a seein' 'bout everything. He was good to his slaves but he had 'em whipped now an' den. De whippin' was alwa's purty tough as dey used ho'se whips an' long switches. Dey was stripped off to de waist an' tied to a tree an' whipped. Now I never seed a whippin' block or whar dey was put in stock, but I'se heard my pappy tell o' how de slave buyers would come through and de slaves would be lined up in long rows an' marched up to a cross rood generally, an' put up fer sale. Sometimes dey would bring a good price ob several hundred dollars, den dey was took off to no tellin' whar an' folks would never know ob 'em no mo'.

"My pappy done fiel' wuk in season but de mos' ob de time he was de shoe maker fer all de slaves on Marse's three plantations. Dat kept him busy mos' ob de time. De shoes was made from rough cow hide wid brass on put on de toes to keep 'em from wearin' out so soon. When de slaves was give a pair ob dem shoes he knowed dey sho' had to las' a long time. Now de clothes dey wore was lak de shoes plain an' course. Dey had to wear mos' anything dey could git deir han's on. I'se heard my pa say dat dey had to wash 'en on Saturday nights an' dry 'em by de fire. Dey wore 'bout de same things on Sundays jes' washed up a bit. Deir wasn't no whar to go much back in dem days on Sundays only to Church 'bout one Sunday out ob each month. De slaves mos' an' generally was tired out an lay 'round 'an rested.

"Back in dem days de darkies wasn't never gibe no book learnin' to amount to anything an' not knowin' much dey couldn't understand much 'bout things an' was terrible superstitious. My pappy an' mammy believed in haints, ghos' an' hoo doo. Dey watched all kinds o' queer signs an' believed in 'em. Dey would tell hair raisin' tales ob hob gobblins an' things dey was scared ub. I recollect one time my ma was gwine through a fiel' one bright moon light night. She was already scart an' excited an' expecting some 'em when she say she looked a little ways across de fiel's an' seed a man wid long white hair a swingin' 'round in de moon light. She say it looked lak he jes' flooted 'long instead ob walkin', he looked bright eyed an' sad. He kept a gittin' closer an' closer to her. She knowed he was a ghos' as she could see slap through 'em. She say she ran as fas' as she could a screamin' till she got to de slave cabins an' was scart to look back to see if he was still a followin' her.

"I met Melinda at Church on Sunday. Me or her neither had no notion ob gittin' married, but I laked her looks, she was purty an' a bright yellow. I courted an' sparked her, went to her house an' walked about wid her till we decided to git married. Now a heap o' boys tried to beat my time wid her but I was de lucky fellow. We had a grand weddin' an' had a big supper an' frolic dat night. We had plenty ob dancin' wid fiddle music an' an accordian playin' an' darkies singin' dem ole songs ob long ago. Dey was a few white folks at our weddin' cermony but ob course dey didn't stay fo' de frolic. Melinda sho was dressed up purty fo' de weddin'. She was all in white wid lace, ribbons an' flowers. She did look good to me. We raised nine chillun an' gibe 'em some education. Dey has made good farmers an' all is doing very well. Melanie an' me wuked hard an' got our home an' tried to alwa's keep it fixed up. My hobby in life was to be a home builder. I has alwa's liked to hunt an' fish. In my yound days I danced an' sung a heap but fer years I'se been too ole but I leans on my Church. Melinda has been dead fifteen years an' I ain't never married no mo'.

"De young colored folks ob dis day ain't a 'mountin' to nothin'. Dey is wild, rough an' uneducated. Dey could git educated if dey wanted to but dey jes' ain't a doin' it.

My great-great-grandfather sounds like he was a prophet because it sure appears he was describing some folks today.

In the 1950s the Mississippi Highway Department expanded Interstate Highway 49, which went through Mendenhall, Simpson County, Mississippi. Part of that expansion went straight through the cemetery where Antney Hays, his wife, and the White families were buried. During the construction of Interstate Highway 49, it was decided that all the White graves would be exhumed and moved. Antney Hays and his wife were not moved and to this day are the only two graves still on the banks of Interstate Highway 49 in Simpson County, Mississippi.

My dad had always wanted to have their graves exhumed and moved to the local Black church cemetery that he had helped to establish, but I disagreed. I believe their graves are a very vital and an important part of Mississippi and American history. I believe and will work to get the state of Mississippi to declare their graves as a historical landmark.

My dad never got a chance to see this accomplished during his life, but I hope and pray to see this done within my lifetime. I recently wrote letters to the two Mississippi United States senators in Washington, DC, requesting their help in getting this accomplished. I guess like most African American concerns in Mississippi, I never got a response from either senator.

Our search for our ancestors was almost impossible without any written records. We were unable to find any records of any family members of the Hays family before Antney Hays. Very few African American that I am aware of—except for perhaps Alex Haley, the author of Roots, and a few others—can trace their family history beyond the emancipation. We were at a dead end until my younger brother Greg, who was probably a little smarter than the rest of us, realized that there had to be records kept for slaves somewhere.

The records for slaves were not kept in the Bureau of Vital Statistics like other people because at the time, slaves were not considered people. They were considered property, like livestock. The records of slaves were kept under the Slave Master's Property List or Slave Schedule. Greg was able through his research to locate the Slave Master's Property Schedule for slave master William Hays, and there it was, the history of the Hays family—my family.

William Hays, a White slave plantation owner and slave trader, had purchased my grandfather's grandfather from some slave traders in Virginia. William Hays moved his slaves from Virginia to Simpson County, Mississippi, where decades later I was born and many of my relatives still live today. Greg was able to locate the William Hays property / bill of sales list for slaves William Hays owned. According to the slave schedule for William Hays, in 1850, William Hays owned fifteen slaves.

That property list / slave schedule had the names of our direct ancestors. Like Alex Haley, Greg had found "our roots."

I often hear African Americans complain about American historians and the way they have recorded American history. Many African Americans complain about the way most American history writers have neglected to include much of the contributions of African Americans.

I agree with those complaints with one exception, and that exception is, why do African Americans have to wait for someone else to record their contributions to American history? There are highly distinguishable African American historians and professors at some of the top colleges and universities in America. Why don't they write and teach about the contributions of African Americans?

I don't know a lot about my ancestors on my mother's side of the family. I knew my mother's father, mother, and her two brothers, and that's about all. I know a little bit more about my ancestors on my father's side of the family, and I am going to write and record as much as I can about them so that my children, grandchildren, nieces, nephews, and all others that would like to know about the contributions of the Hays family to American history will be able to read about it.

After finding my roots and understanding why many slaves were treated in such inhumane ways, I now understand a lot more about why my grandfather and other Black men during my grandfather's time acted and did some of the things they did. I now understand why I rarely witnessed my grandfather who was a first-generation born free in our family showed very little affection for my grandmother or his children.

My grandfather had learned from his slave-born father not to show very much affection for a family member because that could get them sold or traded to another plantation. This was another way the slave master kept their slaves from having any family ties.

My dad was only a second generation from this type of upbringing. He had to learn how to be affectionate to his family, not from what he had experienced at home like most children should learn today, but by the teaching of his godly mother. My grandmother was a godly woman who taught her family to abandon the slave mentality and adopt and live by Christian principles.

Just as the effects of the physical abuse of slavery have been passed genetically to several generations, it follows that the emotional and psychological effects have too. There have been many studies done to determine why there are more proportionately African American single-parent families than most other American families or why there are more African Americans proportionately in prison than most other Americans. I believe it can partially be traced back to the genetically passed genes of the emotional and psychological effects of slavery and the racial injustice after slavery and in many cases even today.

My grandfather didn't finish high school, but he earned and possessed many degrees.

My grandfather's behavior was very common for most African Americans born during and shortly after slavery. He was an honest, hardworking man. My grandfather had a lot of faults because of the after-effects of slavery, but he also had a lot of good qualities. Studies reveal that just as bad genes are passed generationally, so are good ones.

I was recently honored by being invited to be the keynote commencement speaker for a local college graduating class. I attempted to illustrate and explain to the graduates in my speech how they would soon be walking out of the halls of their college receiving many various degrees. I attempted to explain to them, there were many degrees their school would be bestowing on them as they walked across the stage.

I also tried to illustrate and explain to them that there were many other degrees just as important or more important than the one their school would be awarding. I tried to illustrate and explain to the graduating class that my grandfather did not receive any college degrees during his life or even a high school diploma. But he earned, lived by, and taught his family about degrees that are sometimes much more important than any degree any school could award.

I told the class, "My grandfather earned and lived by a high degree of integrity, which is just as important as any bachelor of science degree. The degree of honesty, which is just as important as the bachelor of arts degree. The degree of self-respect, which is just as important as the PhD degree. My grandfather had a high degree of common sense, a high degree of self-respect that he passed on to his children and grandchildren.

My grandfather's degrees were not earned in the classroom but were earned in the everyday walk of life. I tried to illustrate and explain to the graduates that they should also strive to earn in addition to their academic degrees some of the degrees my grandfather earned.

My father grew up in a home where his father hardly ever went to church. His father worked hard Monday through Friday, and from what I remember of him, he got drunk every Saturday and stayed drunk until Monday. My dad and his four brothers and four sisters were probably influenced by their father and had to overcome some unfortunate situations because of my granddad's drinking problems.

A Black man getting drunk on Saturday and staying drunk until Monday was very common during my grandfather's day. There was very little else a Black man could do after working hard all week to relieve the stress of his day. I guess what's most important is, most of these hardworking Black men would only get drunk on weekends and be ready for another hard week by Monday. There were some, however, who were not strong enough to deal with stress and allowed alcohol to control them.

All of my dad's brothers generally had to work hard not to follow the lifestyle they had been taught by their father. They all worked hard Monday through Friday and tried to follow the teachings of their mother. Alcohol abuse created some real family problems in many cases.

My dad despised the use of alcohol as a way to deal with stress and problems. He was always criticizing his father and his brothers for their use and abuse of alcohol. My dad would not allow his father, his brothers, or anyone else to come around our home if they had been drinking. He most certainly would not allow any of his children to use or be around anyone consuming alcohol.

So how could my dad, who grew up experiencing an alcoholic father, become a person God could use to influence his children and others and to teach them by example not to abuse alcohol and end up in a broken home and not to use any excuse for not being able to succeed? My dad had to endure some very dark days in his life, but he believed and taught his children, "The darker your path, the brighter your light can shine."

God never calls a person to perform a task without providing someone or something to guide or assist them with the call he has made on their lives. "God does not call the qualified; God qualifies the ones he calls" (Dr. Larry Mercer).

For Noah, it was a boat. For Moses, it was a rod. For David, it was a stone. For Abraham, it was a ram. "God is faithful; he will not let you be tempted beyond what you can bear" (1 Cor. 10:13). God also did not let my dad bear more than he could but provided a guide for him.

My dad's guide was his God-sent mother, who was the epitome of a godly woman. She was submissive and faithful to her sometimes alcoholic, abusive husband. She loved and tried to raise her children and grandchildren in a godly manner. She made sure they all went to church, and most of all, she constantly prayed for them. Her prayers transcended her children to her many grandchildren. I am truly a product of my grandmother's prayers even to this day.

My dad followed most of the teachings of his godly mother rather than following many of the ways of his father. I am sure it was very difficult for him to step outside his comfort zone and not be like his father, who sometimes was an alcoholic, abusive husband to my father's mother or to abuse alcohol like so many others would have done under the circumstances, but he was able to step outside his comfort zone and answer the call God had planned for him.

I often wondered growing up at my father's table how a man who never had a godly father role model and had no training or teaching on how to be a good husband and father could have done as well as my father. He was the first and only male in his family to attend college. He was always concerned not only for his own family but also for his mother, father, sisters and brothers, their children, and other people in the community that looked up to him for guidance.

Growing Up at My Dad's Table

Growing up as a child, I thought my dad was very demanding, harsh, and unforgiving. My siblings and I were not generally allowed to hang out with most of the other children in the community. During the school year, we were not allowed to watch television except on weekends. We had to be in bed because of an eight o'clock curfew on school nights and a ten o'clock curfew on nonschool nights.

We were not allowed to attend dances or nightclubs or even go around any place where alcohol was sold or consumed. We always had chores and responsibilities to perform that were designed to help support the family and keep us out of trouble.

When I return home on visits today and see some of the places and people I so badly wanted to go and so badly wanted to hang out with and now see where they are today, I now understand why my dad did not allow me to go or hang out with them. We were not allowed to hang out with certain people, but we were also not allowed to look down on them. My dad taught us that people are not always responsible for their circumstances. He taught us that regardless of their situation, they are still God's creation.

I guess good parents can generally see what children can't see. I only regret I never took the time to tell my dad how much I appreciated the way he raised me. There is no greater joy I have experienced than the joy I feel when my daughter Sabrina often tells me, "Thank you for the way you raised me." I guess being a young mom and a public school teacher helps her to better understand how important it is to raise children the right way.

We were severely disciplined, especially the six boys, for violating my dad's rules. I now know my dad was just trying the best he knew how to raise his family to be successful and godly. My dad was far from being a perfect man, but now considering what he had to overcome, he was a remarkable man. He made each one of his eight children feel they were very special and could accomplish anything in life we wanted to through God's will.

My father taught his children godly Christian principles, and I can never remember a week that went by when my dad didn't call us together as a family at the dinner table and pray for each one of us. He tried to make sure we understood we were God's creation and God had a special purpose for each one of us. He made sure we were made to feel special.

We grew up in financial poverty but rich in love and faith. My dad made us believe we were as wealthy as anyone. We lived below the poverty level, but my dad never let us know it. My dad would never consider welfare or any form of government assistance. We had very little to get by on, but he always gave to the church first and taught us to give to the church first out of the little we had.

We were taught to never think anyone was better than we were but to never think we were better than anyone else. I'll never forget my younger brother Dwight. He and I were making fun of some poor children who didn't have decent clothes to wear. I believe that was the worst whipping my dad ever gave my brother and me. And my dad didn't believe in sparing the rod. When it comes to my dad, I wish that was the one verse in the Bible God had left out.

After any discipline of either one of his eight children, my dad would call a prayer meeting for all of us and tried to instill some life principles in us. It didn't matter which one of us was disciplined; we all had to attend the prayer meeting and lecture. One may have gotten the rod, but we all got the lecture that followed. Most of the times, I would have just wished I could have gotten the rod without the lecture.

The lesson he taught us after my brother and I were laughing at the poor children was to "never feel you are better than anyone, and if you do look up, there is always someone higher up than you, but to never feel that you are worse off than anyone, because when you do look down, there is always someone worse off."

My dad loved to use clichés and give illustrations about life. He once told me, "Life is like being on a merry-go-round. If you are on a merry-go-round and you always look in front of you, you are always dead last and a follower, but if you always look behind you, you are in front and everyone is following you because you are a leader." I was always inspired to look behind me and be a leader and not a follower. My dad also taught me that you can always judge a good leader by who is following him.

Many of those prayer meetings and lectures at my daddy's dinner table have been my guide throughout my life. Many difficult decisions I have had to make in life have been based on those dinner-table lectures. My daddy is with the Lord now, but his lectures are still here guiding me and my siblings. "Train up a child in the way he should go, and when he is old, he will not depart" (Proverb 22:6).

Thanks, Dad, for training me up in the way I should go. "You fought a good fight; you kept the faith." We would have loved to have had you around a little longer, but the Lord said you had finished your course, and I am sure you are sporting the crown the Lord had waiting for you (2 Tim. 4:7).

The Damaging Effects of Slavery Still Exist

Steadman Hays, my dad, in my opinion, was most certainly called by God at a special time and to fulfill a special and unique purpose in God's plan. Steadman Hays was born the fourth of eight children to Walter and Annie Hays Sr. in 1918. Steadman Hays's father was a first generation in his family of an African American born free. All my grandfather knew about being a husband and a father was taught to him by his father and other former slaves.

My grandfather became a very successful farmer, businessman, and property owner, but he was also sometimes an abusive alcoholic who had very little formal education. He therefore placed very little emphasis on education. It might have been because there were very few opportunities for an educated Black person at the time.

A Black person at the time had to learn how to survive. Farming was about the only profession for Black people during my grandfather's time. My grandfather might have not had very much formal education, but he was a very wise man and became a very successful farmer, property and business owner.

My grandfather's father, Washington Hays Jr., was born a slave in 1860. Therefore, my grandfather was taught by his father how to be a husband and father during the aftermath of the reality of just how damaging, cruel, and abusive slavery was and how it has affected Black people generationally even to this day. My grandfather learned at the feet of his father. My grandfather's father had learned from his slave father how to be a husband and father.

My father and all his siblings learned most of the principles of life from their mother and father. They learned the good, the bad, and the ugly. My dad's father had been a very successful farmer with hundreds of acres of land, cattle, horses, and rent houses. My dad's father, Walter Hays, at one time owned his own Molasses Manufacturing Company.

One of my dad's brothers, Walter Hays Jr., also became very successful in the construction business. Walter Hays Jr. during his lifetime owned land, a fleet of trucks, heavy-duty Caterpillars, and tractors and had a crew of employees. He always drove a new car and was the first person in my hometown that I remember owning a color television.

Walter Hays Jr. during his younger days was the crown of success and the envy of most people in Mendenhall, Mississippi. Most young boys looked up to him and wanted to be like him. Walter Hays Jr. should have been a millionaire, but because of racism and racist schemes at the time to prevent Blacks from succeeding and the lack of adequate business skills—such as good investments, bookkeeping, accounting—and other proper business requirements, Walter Hays Jr. would die with very little left of his empire except a small amount of land, a house, and maybe a vehicle or two to pass on to his children.

RIP, Uncle Walter Hays Jr.

One of the most damaging things about slavery was not just the physical and brutal way some slaves were treated, but the psychological and emotional trauma they endured whose effects would be passed down genetically. Physical scars are much easier and faster to heal than emotional and psychological ones.

Physical scars may eventually heal, but the emotional and psychological wounds can be passed to the next generation. It does not take a psychiatrist or sociologist to understand these traits can be passed to several generations. This knowledge helps me to understand and appreciate my family much better, even their bad traits.

There are many present-day examples of how the physical abuse of slavery has been passed down through generations. It should also follow that the psychological and emotional abuse has passed through the generations as well. Many African Americans even today still suffer the cruel effects of slavery.

African Americans are more susceptible to many health issues such as hypertension, heart disease, strokes, diabetes, sickle cell, and many others physical and medical conditions than most other Americans. This is probably directly related to the inherited genetics passed from their slave ancestors who were forced to eat unhealthy diets and live in unhealthy living conditions. This goes to show that African Americans are still suffering from the physical effects of slavery.

The emotional and psychological damage was much more severe, lasting, and devastating than the physical that has been genetically passed down from African American slave ancestors. Most slave master would not allow slaves to have family ties or affection for family. This was not good for the slave business.

Just as many African Americans today still suffer from the after-effects of physical abuse that has been passed down genetically from their slave ancestors, I believe the emotional and psychological abuse has been passed down as well. When we read about more than 50 percent of African American homes today are headed by single parents, generally a mother, we should also question why.

We should question where are the African American fathers and why. We should question, why are there more African American males in prison than in college? As a criminal defense attorney and judge for many years, I have often asked the question why. Why are more than 90 percent of the young African Americans that I have had to represent come to court with no father figure in their life?

I am not advocating nor am I suggesting slavery as the only reason for all the dysfunctional African American families, but we must face reality and accept the truth, for "the truth will set you free" (John 8:31–32). I am also not suggesting that a single mother cannot properly raise a child. I have seen some great single mothers that have done great jobs, but according to statistics, in most cases that is not what happens.

If a slave was taught and allowed to love his wife or children, he would probably not stand by and see them abused. So it was easier for the slave master to promote a slave to have women and babies but not have any commitment, affection, attachment, or responsibility for them. This is probably where the term Black stud originated. Slaves were property, like the cattle, and were treated like cattle and other livestock. There were few family values taught or in most cases allowed.

Some slave masters and slave traders used certain slaves for breeding purposes. They would pick the strongest and healthiest slaves for reproduction. This may account for why many African American athletes are stronger and faster than some other Americans. The superior genes were passed down from their slave ancestors.

Family values and ties could create problems for the slave master. When slaves developed affection for one another, they would unite, rise up, and revolt against mistreatment. When the slave master noticed slaves developing relationships, the slave master would generally sell or trade that slave to another plantation to prevent family ties or relationships.

My grandfather was the product of this type of environment. This was at the time the only type of exposure he had experienced and could pass on to his children.

God will sometimes have people to go through a testing period before he can use them. Noah preached the same sermon for forty years about a flood to people who had never seen rain before. Abraham was a hundred years old before God gave him his promised son. Moses wandered in the desert for forty years before God used him. When I look at my dad's life and some of the many obstacles and hardships he had to overcome, I wonder if this was the way God was preparing him for what God had planned for him.

My dad made his family aware of the many disparities, inequities, and discriminatory roadblocks Black people would have to overcome in order to succeed. While these roadblocks were designed to hold Black people back, my dad used them to teach his family to never use them as excuses. He taught us, because of these roadblocks, we had to be better than those that put the roadblocks in front of us. I think Dr. Martin L. King Jr. said it best: "He who gets behind in a race must run faster than the man in front or forever remain behind." Steadman Hays always taught his children not to waste time complaining about the man in front but to use that energy to run faster than the man in front.

Lynching, Police, and Church Leaders

In the 1960s during my formal school years growing up in Mississippi, there were a lot of changes going on across the country. Blacks were standing up demanding their civil rights. My dad, Steadman Hays, took an active role in these changes. He was elected president of the local branch of the NAACP and worked closely with Medgar Evers, the Mississippi State field secretary of the NAACP.

Blacks all over the country were standing up and challenging the Jim Crow laws, the so-called separate but equal laws. People were being called on to step outside their comfort zone to integrate all segregated public facilities such as businesses, jobs, and especially schools.

During this time several of my classmates and I decided to step outside our comfort zone and answer the call to integrate our hometown Mendenhall High School. All public schools at the time were segregated.

The decision to integrate our hometown school did not please a lot of White people.

The KKK in 1964, just a year before my classmates and I had decided to integrate Mendenhall High School, murdered the three civil rights workers—Michael Schwerner, Andrew Goodman, and James Chaney—just a few miles down the road from where my dad was the pastor of a local church. Many others were lynched, and many more were beaten and jailed on frivolous charges just because they took a stand against the injustice Black people faced in Mississippi and most of the South. This was the Mississippi I grew up in as a child. This was the Mississippi my classmates and I were about to take on.

In the 1950s and '60s, Mississippi was a very dangerous place to be if you were Black or White who tried to aid in the struggle for justice and equality for an African American. The dark and gloomy effect of the whole problem was there was no help to be expected from the police or law enforcement, because in many cases, they were the ones wearing the blue by day and the white sheets by night and the main ones doing the beatings and killings or aiding in them.

There was not even any refuge to be expected from most White church leaders or White Christians. There have been a lot of studies done, and it has been reported that in many of the lynchings and murders that took place during the Civil Right Era, White ministers and White church leaders were present and involved.

Steadman Hays, my dad, along with a few other civil rights leaders, began to hold meetings at various churches to teach and strategize ways to deal with the discrimination Black people faced in Mississippi and other parts of the South. Many of these churches would become targets for bombings and attacks by the Klan once they found out about the meetings. Therefore, these meetings had to be moved to homes. Our home became one of the homes where these secret meetings were held. This is when my dad had to teach his family "the Klan drills."

The Klan would drive by to see what homes had more than one car in the driveway. Most families in the '60s had only one family car. If there were more than one car in the driveway of any Black home, that home would probably get a visit from the local Klan. When we had meetings at our home, my dad would have us park the extra cars in the back fields behind our house where they couldn't be seen by a person driving down the road.

The KKK advertising their hate organization and reminding the public what could happen if they got out of line.

Most Klansmen wore sheets and hoods to disguise their identity such as many public officials, law enforcement officers, civic leaders, ministers, and church leaders; but others didn't care and were proud to let their identity be known and was proud of it. They proudly displayed their uniforms like the ones below.

The Klan, in my hometown as well as many other Southern cities, held many public rallies to intimidate those that might disagree with their position. The Klan also held private rallies in secret and secluded locations. Many of the Klan meetings would actually be held in "God's house of prayer"—the church.

My granddad owned a large amount of land that was adjacent to land owned (or had actually been swindled from my granddad) by a White neighbor. One night, my brothers Paul and Dwight; my three cousins Ronnie, Randy, Donnie, and I were hiking through my granddad's pasture. My hometown had no recreation for Black children, so country boys had to find other ways to amuse themselves. On Saturday nights, we would often go hiking through the woods just for amusement.

On this particular night, as we were hiking through the woods, we could see this large campfire in the distance on the White neighbor's property adjacent to my granddad's property. We approached to get a better look at what was going on. As we got closer, we realized it was a massive Klan rally. It looked like every White person in Mendenhall was there.

The Klan didn't just hold rallies and make late nighttime calls on people they wanted to get their message to; they, in many cases, carried out their message in the form of the most barbaric and savage lynching. Lynchings were the way the Klan tried to publicly get their message across.

A Black person would generally be dragged out of his house in the middle of the night. They would then be beaten, tortured, killed, and left hanging on a tree for others to see and be enlightened. My older sister Evelyn often talked about a tree not too far from our childhood home where my grandfather would take her to see the tree and tell her of the many Black people that had been lynched there.

According to records, many of the lynching's were attended by white ministers and White church leaders as observers and participants.

Unfortunately, this was not the only tree where Black people had been lynched. There are many trees throughout the South that if trees could talk, they would tell the many stories of the horrible lynchings they witnessed.

My wife and I recently visited her hometown, Selma, Alabama, where we visited the infamous Edmund Pettus Bridge. The bridge is named after Edmund Winston Pettus, a former Confederate Brigadier General. The bridge became internationally famous during the '60s civil rights era. Dr. Martin L. King Jr. and many other civil rights participants marched across the bridge from Selma on their way to Montgomery, Alabama's state capitol after what became known as "Bloody Sunday."

On March 7, 1965 (Bloody Sunday), marchers were beaten with billy clubs, tear gassed, and trampled with horses. People in America and around the world could not believe the evil they saw demonstrated by law enforcement. America witnessed little children and women trampled by horses simply because they wanted equal rights. People around the world saw with disbelief for the first time what many Blacks had seen and been exposed to for years.

On Sunday, March 21, 1965, Dr. Martin L. King Jr., after securing a court order to march, started out with a little over three thousand marchers headed for the infamous Edmund Pettus Bridge. The marchers traveled about twelve miles per day on their way to Montgomery under federal protection. The marchers were joined with celebrities and people from all over the world. By the time the marchers reached Montgomery on Thursday, March 25, their number had grown to over twenty-five thousand. This march brought about the signing of the Voting Rights Act by President Lyndon B. Johnson.

As my wife and I stood at the foot of the infamous Edmund Pettus Bridge, I could only imagine the horror those marchers must have experienced on Bloody Sunday. But more shocking is to believe this horror was being inflicted by the people that had taken an oath to protect them—"the police." While this may be shocking to some, it was not shocking to me because I had lived much of my life being made very much aware that those that wore the blue by day also wore the sheets by night.

The plaque below is situated at the foot of the entrance to the infamous Edmund Pettus Bridge to remind the world just how true this was. Selma was just one of the many examples of how those in the blue by day were those in sheets by night. This is also one of the reasons many Black people don't trust police officers even today.

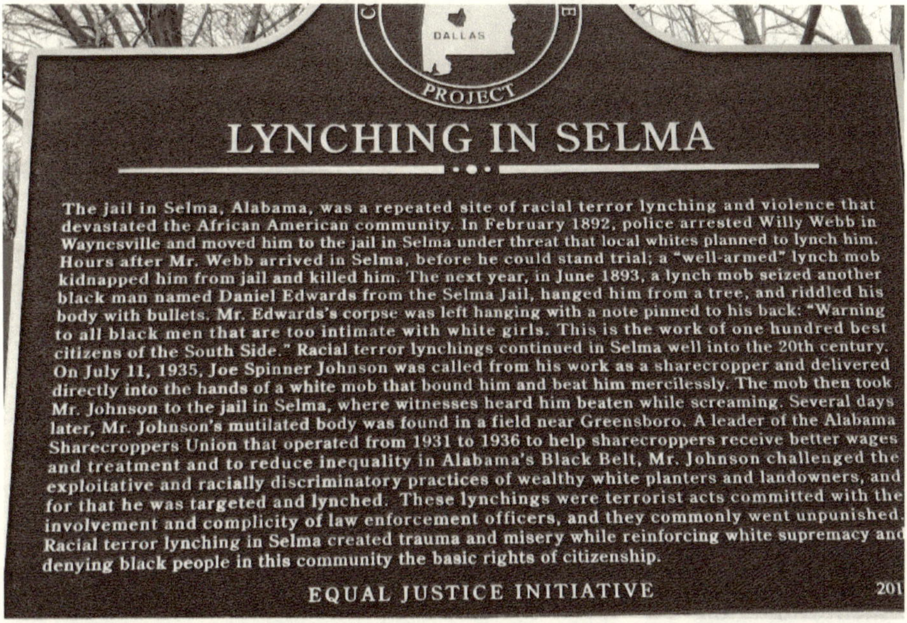

DALLAS
PROJECT
LYNCHING IN SELMA
The jail in Selma, Alabama, was a repeated site of racial terror lynching and violence that devastated the African American community. In February 1892, police arrested Willy Webb in Waynesville and moved him to the jail in Selma under threat that local whites planned to lynch him. Hours after Mr. Webb arrived in Selma, before he could stand trial; a "well-armed" lynch mob kidnapped him from jail and killed him. The next year, in June 1893, a lynch mob seized another black man named Daniel Edwards from the Selma Jail, hanged him from a tree, and riddled his body with bullets. Mr. Edwards's corpse was left hanging with a note pinned to his back: "Warning to all black men that are too intimate with white girls. This is the work of one hundred best citizens of the South Side." Racial terror lynchings continued in Selma well into the 20th century. On July 11, 1935, Joe Spinner Johnson was called from his work as a sharecropper and delivered directly into the hands of a white mob that bound him and beat him mercilessly. The mob then took Mr. Johnson to the jail in Selma, where witnesses heard him beaten while screaming. Several days later, Mr. Johnson's mutilated body was found in a field near Greensboro. A leader of the Alabama Sharecroppers Union that operated from 1931 to 1936 to help sharecroppers receive better wages and treatment and to reduce inequality in Alabama's Black Belt, Mr. Johnson challenged the exploitative and racially discriminatory practices of wealthy white planters and landowners, and for that he was targeted and lynched. These lynchings were terrorist acts committed with the involvement and complicity of law enforcement officers, and they commonly went unpunished. Racial terror lynching in Selma created trauma and misery while reinforcing white supremacy and denying black people in this community the basic rights of citizenship.
EQUAL JUSTICE INITIATIVE

My dad witnessed many aftermaths of lynchings during his life. He, along with some other civil rights leaders, did a study on lynchings and discovered that many lynchings were attended by many of the civic leaders, law enforcement officers, ministers, and church leaders. There was one lynching that had taken place in my hometown a few years earlier where the main civic leaders in the city led the mob that kicked in this Black man's house in the middle of the night, dragged him out in front of his wife and screaming children, and brutally beat, tortured, hanged, and killed him.

One of the civic leaders was the owner of the major and most popular supermarket where most people in my hometown shopped. My dad never allowed us to go into that store again. He became very unpopular with many of the White citizens, especially the business owners, when he led a demonstration and boycott against that store owner and any other business owners that discriminated against Blacks.

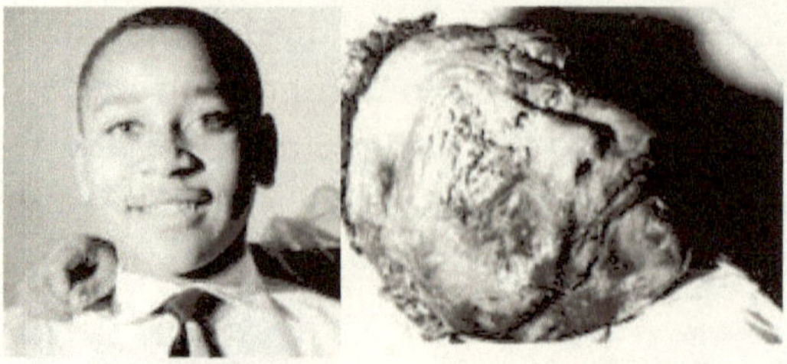

Fourteen-year-old Emmitt Till

Just a few years prior to my dad's protest and boycott for the Black man in my hometown who had been lynched by the mob led by the civic leader and supermarket owner, fourteen-year-old Emmitt Till, who left Chicago in August 1955 to visit relatives in Mississippi for his summer vacation, was dragged out of his great-uncle's house and was barbarically killed after being brutally and savagely beaten beyond recognition. His face was so mutilated and disfigured to the point that both eyes were beaten out of their sockets.

This all happened because Carolyn Bryant, a White twenty-one-year-old employee of her family's small grocery store, was probably having a bad day, so she claimed young Till whistled at her. While this may not seem to be a big thing, but in Mississippi in those days, a Black man could be lynched for just looking at a White woman. Many Black men would hold their heads down in the presence of a White woman so they could not be accused of looking at one.

The shameful truth is that nothing was done, and nothing would have been done to the murderers of Emmitt Till had it not been for the national outrage after seeing the tortured remains of Till at his funeral. This forced the state of Mississippi to at least pretend to seek some resemblance of justice by bringing the murderers to trial in front of an all-White Mississippi jury. No one was surprised when the all-White jury failed to return a guilty verdict.

Years later, Carolyn Bryant, Till's accuser, admitted she had lied on Till. The men who had been acquitted by the all-White Mississippi jury later sold their story to a national magazine admitting they had in fact lynched and murdered Emmitt Till.

This was the kind of justice an African American could expect in the state of Mississippi when I was growing up there. This was the kind of reality my dad, Steadman Hays, had been called upon to step outside his comfort zone to bring attention to. It wasn't just stepping outside his comfort zone; it was stepping into the danger zone.

My dad witnessed much injustice in Mississippi inflicted on others as well as injustice he personally experienced. He witnessed his father having land taken by a White neighbor and the so-called justice system did nothing about it. My dad worked on jobs where he and other Blacks were paid less than their White coworkers and the so-called justice system did nothing about it. My dad witnessed the humiliation his wife and many other African Americans faced when they tried to vote. My dad witnessed lynchings and other racial injustice, but never once do I recall my dad ever teaching his children revenge or hatred for our oppressors. My dad always taught his children to trust in God for God always had the last say.

James Chaney Andrew Goodman Michael Schwerner

Then, in 1964 three young men were willing to risk the danger by stepping outside their comfort zone went to Mississippi, probably one of the most dangerous and hateful places in the world, to aid in securing the civil rights of all people.

The three had gone to Neshoba County, Mississippi, ironically next door to a city called Philadelphia (city of brotherly love) to aid in registering Black people to vote. This did not sit well with the Mississippi racist White Klan community. Cecil Price, a devout Klansman and sheriff of Neshoba County, Mississippi, had the three arrested on some trumped-up frivolous traffic violation charges. Sheriff Price held the activists in jail until he and his Klan friends could set up a plot to kidnap and murder the young men.

The young men were released from jail and told to follow the sheriff who was to escort them out of town. Sheriff Price had prearranged for the Klan and other local police agencies to intercept the civil right activists and murdered them. The activists were murdered and buried under a road construction dam. Their bodies probably would have never been found, as was the case with so many people that disappeared in Mississippi, had it not been for the payoff of a paid informant.

The informant three months later told where the bodies could be found and who was involved in their abduction, murder, and cover-up. The informant stated that the murders were done by the local White knights of the Ku Klux Klan, the Neshoba County Sheriff's Office, and the Philadelphia Mississippi Police Department.

The state of Mississippi refused to prosecute any of the murderers. Three years later, after national and world public outrage, the federal government filed charges against eighteen individuals with civil rights violations. Seven were convicted and received relatively minor sentences for the civil rights violations.

In 1964 when those activists were killed, my dad pastored a local church just a few miles from where those young men were killed. My dad often talked about the racial tension and how Black people were being scrutinized in the city. He remembered there were always spies, mainly law enforcement, watching his church, especially when the church had a function that was held at night or was held on any day that was not Sunday. Many of my dad's Black members were afraid to attend church at night.

My dad, along with other Black leaders, called for a federal investigation into the killing of the three civil rights leaders because it was well understood, Mississippi would do nothing or very little to prosecute anyone for killing a Black person or a White person who was trying to assist in civil rights.

A year prior to the three civil rights workers' murder, on Sunday Morning, September 9, 1963, four little girls went to church and were murdered by some racist deranged White Klansmen. This is what was left of God's church after the dynamite exploded. Four little girls were killed, and many more church attendees were injured.

In 1961 young Freedom Riders stepped outside their comfort zone and boarded buses all over the North to go South to challenge the Jim Crow laws of the South. Many were met with hatred and violence but could not seek help from the police or other law enforcement agencies that were sworn to protect them. In many cases, the local police and other law enforcement agencies were members of the hate groups like the Klan, and in other cases the local police and other law enforcement agencies were part of the mobs that were inflicting the violence against them.

In many cases, the bus drivers would alert the local Ku Klux Klan as to their route and arrival time so that the Klan could be ready to intercept the Freedom Riders with hatred and violence. One bus driver pulled into one of the southern bus terminals and stated to the angry awaiting mob that he had brought them a busload of Niggers and Nigger lovers. The local police in some cases would conveniently find themselves on another assignment across town so that the Klan and angry mobs would have full access to the Freedom Riders. In many other cases, the police and local law enforcement would just stand by and do nothing while the mobs beat the Freedom Riders. Still in other cases the police and local law enfrcement agencies would be part of the angry mob. Many Freedom Riders were severely beaten. In many cases, Freedom Riders would be charged and jailed on frivious charges.

The Freedom Riders were trained to be nonviolent regardless of whether they were attacked. This policy made it easy and covenient for cowards to attack them. In one case, the Klan attempted to burn a whole busload of Freedom Riders including women and children alive.

Medgar Evers

On June 12, 1963, Medgar Evers, a well-educated, articulate, honored military veteran, was gunned down and murdered in his driveway. Evers, who had defended his country by fighting in France and Germany during World War II, attracted the attention of many people concerning the injustice in his home state of Mississippi. Evers was a threat to the status quo of the Jim Crow laws and had to be dealt with Mississippi-style because he was willing to step outside his comfort zone to assist people being mistreated.

Evers became the first field secretary of the NAACP in Mississippi. He became very effective in organizing boycotts of segregated businesses. Evers also organized voter registration classes across the state of Mississippi for Black people that had been denied the right to vote in Mississippi. He became a target for a lot of radical hate groups.

In 1954, Evers applied for admission to attend law school at Mississippi State University. His application was denied because the University of Mississippi would not admit Black students regardless of the fact that Evers had put his life on the line defending his country. Thurgood Marshall would become Evers's attorney in a suit against the University of Mississippi. Later that year the US Supreme Court would hand down a decision in *Brown v. The Board of Education*, which struck down racial discrimination for admission to public schools. This decision gave way for James Meredith to become the first African American to be admitted to the University of Mississippi in 1962.

Evers continued his efforts to seek equality for all Americans in Mississippi and also lobbied to reopen the murder case of Emmitt Till. Then on June 12, 1963, after giving what my older sister Evelyn said was one of the most eloquent and compassionate speeches for justice she had ever heard, Medgar Evers was gunned down in his driveway. He had just returned home from making his famous speech. My dad had also attended the speech that night.

A few minutes after Medgar Evers was gunned down, my dad, who had attended the meeting with Evers, returned home and was preparing for bed when he received two phone calls. The first call was from a friend and fellow civil rights leader who informed my dad of the Evers shooting. The second call was from an anonymous caller who said, "Nigger, you are next." That was the beginning of the many anonymous threatening hate calls the Hays family would endure over the next few years.

Byron De La Beckwith, a White segregationist and founding member of the Mississippi White Citizen Council, became a prime suspect in Evers's murder. Beckwith's gun was found near the murder scene. There were witnesses that put Beckwith near the murder scene and other overwhelming evidence including Beckwith's fingerprints being found on the gun, but two separate all-White Mississippi juries failed to convict him.

Beckwith became somewhat of a celebrity in the state of Mississippi among the racist and segregationist. Beckwith even had the governor of Mississippi, Ross Barnett, to walk into the courtroom during his trial for murdering Medgar Evers and shook Beckwith's hand in front of the judge and jury hearing the case.

The murder of Medgar Evers outraged, energized, and motivated a lot of people to carry on the works of Medgar Evers. My dad had been a close friend, admirer, and coworker of Medgar Evers, intensified his efforts to get African Americans involved in the movement for civil rights. This also made my dad a target. There were numerous times my dad and my brothers who were old enough to hold a gun had to stand off the Klan when they would make their late-night appearances at my dad's door.

America in the '60s went through probably one of the darkest periods in American history, except maybe the Civil War. There was turmoil and racial tension to the point of almost another civil war. Civil rights activist Medgar Evers was assassinated, civil rights activist Malcolm X was assassinated, President John F. Kennedy was assassinated, civil rights activist / Nobel Peace Prize winner Dr. Martin L. King was assassinated, Senator /US Attorney General / presidential candidate Robert Kennedy was assassinated, and thousands of others were killed for their efforts to "secure the blessings of liberty for all."

The country appeared to be as much divided on the racial equality issue in the '60s as was the division just prior to the Civil War. Southern politicians campaigned on segregationist platforms. Governor George Wallace of Alabama, Governor Ross Barnett of Mississippi, Governor Orval Faubus of Arkansas, Governor Lester Maddox of Georgia sold autographed pick handles to beat African Americans and others who attempted to integrate segregated businesses, and other Southern politicians used the racial tension to promote their campaigns. Governor George Wallace and Governor Ross Barnett would later defy the federal law by standing in the doorway of the University of Alabama and the University of Mississippi to prevent the integration of those universities.

This type of bigotry and racial hatred propelled a bullet, as one writer said, that was motivated, guided, and gained momentum by the selfish disregard for human decency and respect for human life and safety by Southern politicians that found its mark with Medgar, Malcolm,

John, Martin, Robert, and thousands of others that stepped outside their comfort zone to try to get this country to respect everyone's right to life, liberty, and the pursuit of happiness.

In the '60s, anyone that crossed the line to speak up for those basic God-given human rights found themselves a target for that bullet. My dad, Steadman Hays, had long been an advocate for civil rights. He had led protests and boycotts against businesses that practiced segregation. He had led a protest against an employer that paid African Americans less than their White counterpart for the same job. He was successful in getting that same company held liable for paying African Americans less than the national minimum wage.

My dad, Steadman Hays, had many people he looked up to and admired. He probably never understood Malcolm X and therefore didn't support what my dad called Malcolm's radical agenda. My dad did not follow Malcolm's philosophy about "by any means necessary." He did not buy totally into the Dr. Martin L. King's nonviolence approach either but believed violence should be a last resort to defend and protect the family. He defended his family and taught all his boys how to operate a gun and to also defend the family when and if necessary.

Unlike my dad, I believed, admired, and followed the teachings of both Dr. Martin L. King Jr. and Malcolm X. I believe both were attempting to accomplish liberation for Blacks but just from different perspectives. Dr. King was trying to help liberate Black people from the visible external bondage, which can be accomplished through legislation. Malcolm was trying to liberate Black people from the invisible bondage, which can only be accomplished through educating the mind. Malcolm realized many African Americans were willing to accept second-class citizenship because they had a slave mentality and didn't know any better.

Dr. King was very successful in helping to get legislation passed for the Voting Rights Act as well as the Civil Rights Act. These were some tremendous accomplishments for Dr. King. Malcolm X on the other hand was able to get Black people to understand how their slave masters and White racists had caused them to accept a three-fourth human mentality. Before Malcolm X, African Americans had no identity and would accept anything except being Black. Black was a derogatory term that most African Americans did not want to be identified with.

This was the main reason African Americans went so many years wondering about their identity. Some African Americans preferred to be referred to as "Colored," "Negro," "Soul Brother," "Afro-American," anything except that beautiful Black person God had made them. Malcolm X did a tremendous job in helping to get African Americans to be proud of what and how God had created them.

I remember the many times the Klan came to our door but my dad would meet them with his guns and let them know he was not going to be the only dead person once the shooting started but would take as many Klansmen with him as he could. As each of my dad's boys got old enough to learn how to use and shoot a gun, we were taught how and would take our stand to back my dad up with our guns at the door whenever the Klan made their call. We were able to back the Klan down each time they made a call at my dad's house.

My dad loved and admired John and Robert Kennedy. He had been a close friend and coworker with Medgar Evers and was with him at the meeting the night Medgar Evers was assassinated. Medgar Evers and my dad had worked closely together on many issues in Mississippi. My older brother Steadman Jr. had actually worked for Mr. Evers. Medgar Evers was the state field secretary of the NAACP, and my dad was one of the local presidents. He also loved and admired Dr. Martin L. King Jr. and had been at many meetings with my mother in Memphis the night Dr. King was assassinated.

My dad's associations and his involvement in civil rights most certainly made him a target. The Hays family lived in constant fear that the same bullet that had found its mark on so many others would someday find its mark on my dad, the outspoken Steadman Hays. Over the next few years, my dad and the Hays family received many death threats and annoying phone calls, but God still had work for Steadman Hays to finish.

Integration of Mendenhall High School

My dad had tried to do what he could to promote justice for all in his community but had also tried to keep his family and children away from the danger that being involved could create. This was what was going on across the country when a few of my classmates and I decided to step outside our comfort zone and signed up to integrate our hometown,

Mendenhall High School. My dad admired me for wanting to get involved but feared for my safety.

There were still other problems that came about after I decided to integrate my high school. My dad was told that if I integrated and attended Mendenhall High rather than the Black high school, he would lose his contract in the state of Mississippi. He had been issued a contract to provide eggs from our poultry farm in the state of Mississippi. In order to secure the contract, my dad had to mortgage everything including our home. Losing this contract would mean we would lose everything. My family would be homeless. I never saw my dad so deflated and depressed.

My dad often unilaterally made all the decisions for his family. This time my dad called me to his side and told me, "Son, it is up to you to decide what to do." I was afraid and fearful for what could happen to me if I integrated the all-White school but not as much afraid for what could happen to my family.

I could not make a decision that would cause the pain and suffering that would come to my dad, mother, and five siblings. It was more painful for my dad to see me make that decision than it was for me. I sadly made the decision to withdraw my name as a candidate to integrate Mendenhall High School.

There were many other issues and problems African Americans faced in Mississippi and the South other than segregation. The right to vote was one of the major ones. In 1965, President Lyndon Johnson, after much pressure from the civil rights movement, signed into law the Voting Rights Act. This was supposed to be a major blow to the segregated South and especially the state of Mississippi. While Blacks made up most of the population in many cities in Mississippi, they were not allowed to vote because of racist schemes like the poll tax, and if a Black person could afford to pay the poll tax, then they had to pass a literacy test. There were many cities in Mississippi where only about 2 percent of the Black citizens voted.

I will never forget the embarrassment my mother went through when she first attempted to vote in Mississippi. My mother was asked to interpret Article 1, Section 3 of the Mississippi State Constitution in order to pass her literacy test. My mother was so embarrassed and humiliated that she never attempted to vote again until the abolishment of the literacy test.

It has been reported that other Blacks in Mississippi were given even more difficult and idiotic literacy test. One Black person reported he was told, in order to pass his literacy test, he had to tell how many drops of water the Mississippi River contained. Another was reportedly asked to state how many bubbles a bar of Ivory soap would produce. There was no way Mississippi was going to allow Blacks the right to vote without a fight.

Medgar Evers and others including my dad, with the help of the Freedom Riders, a few years earlier had decided to take on the state of Mississippi and help Blacks overcome the Mississippi Literacy Tests. There would be literacy test classes taught at various Black churches and in some homes to teach Black people how to pass the literacy test to vote. Several churches and homes were selected.

My dad's home was one of the homes that the classes would be taught in. He taught the classes that were scheduled at our home. Black people would come to our home every Tuesday and Thursday night for voter literacy classes. Our yard would be full of cars until some Klansmen found out what was going on. We then had another visit from our friends in the white sheets.

After that my dad would have us park the cars in the back fields behind our house, hiding them so that the local White neighbors would not know what was going on. If the White neighbors had known what was going on at my dad's house, we would have had another visit from the organization that made the night rides dressed in the white sheets.

In addition to trying to get people registered to vote and teaching them how to vote, many others were taking on the segregated public facilities such as transportation, hotels, restaurants, and public education. I was not old enough to vote, so I set my sights on public education.

Klan Drills

My dad, Steadman Hays, truly was a man who taught his family how to step outside their comfort zone to accomplish their goals. While most parents taught their children and practiced fire drills, storm drills, or other catastrophic types of emergency drills on how to survive during an emergency, Steadman Hays, my dad, taught his children Klan drills.

What are Klan drills? Ask anyone of Steadman Hays's children, and anyone of them can tell you, for we are all experts on Klan drills.

It could be very dangerous growing up in Mississippi in the 1950s and 1960s as I did unless you understood the codes and how a Black person was supposed to respond. It was more commonly called a Black person knowing their place and staying in their place. Blacks either lived by the code, or their life and the lives of their loved ones could be in danger.

Steadman Hays understood the code but refused to accept being treated like a second-class citizen. He might step off the sidewalk, which was what a Black person was supposed to do when a White person approached to allow a White lady to pass but refused to step off the sidewalk just because a White man approached as was the code.

Steadman Hays refused to say "Yes, sir" to a White man half my dad's age when addressing him just because he was White. In many cases, a Black person was considered being disrespectful if they didn't step off the sidewalk when a White person passed by or didn't address a White person as "Sir" or even fail to look down when talking to a White person. A Black person looking directly at a White person when talking to them was considered being disrespectful.

There were many times I personally witnessed my dad telling some young White person he understood his place but was not going to be disrespected as a person. I recall one incident where this young White boy came out to put gas in my dad's car, and when he was finished, he asked my dad, "Uncle, is there anything else you need?" My dad responded by saying, "Your mama is not my sister, so I am not your uncle." Calling a Black man uncle was a way of degrading and disrespect.

These were the codes that Blacks needed to know and follow in order to survive in many places in the South. My dad understood these codes but refused to follow them or do anything that was degrading or disrespectful to him as a man that had been created by a holy God. He also refused to do business and encouraged other Blacks not to do business with companies and businesses that discriminated and required Blacks to humiliate themselves by going through the back door to be served. This went against the code and made Steadman Hays a target.

Steadman Hays found himself constantly having to teach his children how to survive by escaping out the back door in total darkness into the woods behind our house during the many trips the Klan made to our home because he had violated the code. Now you know what a Klan drill is. During the civil rights of the 1960s, we had many Klan drills at my house.

The earliest Klan drill I can remember was when I was no more than three or four years old. I didn't know until years later when it was explained to me what was going on back then by my older sister Evelyn. She had to tell me years later the story of what was going on during my first Klan drill.

I do remember my dad being chased and running into the house, grabbing my younger brother Dwight, who was just an infant, probably three or four months old, out of the crib and rushing us all into the back room of the house close to the back door because the Klan had chased him through the front.

I remember my dad crying and praying a short prayer and then giving each one of his children a hug as if this was the last time he would see us. I remember him showing us how to turn off all the lights in the house and slipping out the back door into the woods in total darkness. Looking back now, I believe he really did believe it would be the last time he would see his family because there was a large group of Klansmen outside our door that had plans to lynch and kill him that night.

I remember my dad getting his gun and going to the front door, and I remember the horrible yells from the Klan, "Come out here, nigger!" I was too young at the time to have really understood what was going on, but my older sister Evelyn explained it to me years later. I do remember our front yard being full of these men wearing white sheets.

I didn't know until years later when my older sister Evelyn told me that was one of the many times the Klan came to our house to get my dad. I later found out the Klan was upset because my dad had contacted an out-of-town attorney to get back some land a White neighbor had swindled my grandfather out of. Blacks were to follow the code and not supposed to use the court system to challenge Whites.

My father taught all of his family how to maneuver through any room in the house in total darkness and find our way to safety. He would get upset with my mother if she rearranged furniture or left anything in the way that might block our escape route. Maybe my wife and children

I hope will now understand why I get a little upset when things are rearranged or things are left in a passageway in our house today.

In 1964, the Civil Rights Act was passed and signed into law. We thought things were finally going to change in Mississippi. I realized firsthand Fredrick Douglas was correct when he said, "There will be no change without a struggle." The passing of the Civil Rights Act would have had little change in Mississippi if it had not been for people like Medgar Evers and others who had to give up their lives to force and bring about a change.

The passing of the Civil Rights Act was supposed to have meant no more segregation, no more Jim Crow laws. The Civil Rights Act was only words on a piece of paper to the state of Mississippi unless someone was willing to risk their lives to enforce it. Some tried, some died, and many more were beaten and persecuted.

James Meredith, a young Black man, decided he would risk his life and challenge the new law to help bring about a change by attempting to integrate the University of Mississippi. James Meredith became my hero. I decided to follow in his footsteps by also challenging the new civil rights law by integrating Mendenhall High School.

There were two high schools in Mendenhall, one for the White students and one for the Black students. Both schools were substandard. The state of Mississippi did not have the funds to adequately operate one school system but was trying to run two. The Black school was even more substandard because it had always been inferior to the White school.

The Black school had always received secondhand, hand-me-down books and everything else after the White school had discarded them. The Black school had to even adopt the same colors as the White school because the Mendenhall School District would not provide football uniforms and equipment for the Black school, so the Black school got the hand me-down uniforms and football equipment from the White school. Both schools had the same colors so that the Black school could use the same color uniforms.

Several of my classmates and I decided to use the new law to challenge the segregated school system in Mississippi. According to the 1964 Civil Rights Act, a student had the right to attend the school of their choice. Since the Black school was so inferior to the White school, we were all going to sign up to attend the White school in the fall of 1965.

All my classmates that had agreed to sign up to attend the White school never actually signed up but led me to believe they had. I ended up being the only Black student that had officially signed up to attend the all-White school. I was so surprised to find out when the US Marshalls came to my home to interview me and told me that I was the only Black student that had signed up to attend the all-White school in Mendenhall, Mississippi, in the fall of 1965.

There was a lot to be concerned about in Mississippi in the '60s if you were Black and stepped out of line according to the White establishment. Signing up to integrate an all-White school could be one of those concerns. Racial tension was on the rise. Churches were being bombed, fourteen-year-old Emmett Till had been brutally beaten and killed, Freedom Riders were being beaten and killed, Medgar Evers had been killed, lynchings were very common, and Mississippi had the highest number of lynchings in the country followed by Georgia and Texas.

Lynchings were very brutal and inhumane and demonstrated just how cruel and savage one person could be to another. One of the most graphic and inhumane was the lynching of a woman in Georgia, Mary Turner. Mrs. Turner's husband, Hayes Turner, had been murdered by a lynch mob for allegedly committing a crime. Mrs. Turner denied her husband's involvement in the crime. She was lynched because she would not agree that her husband had committed the crime.

Mrs. Turner, an eight-month pregnant woman, was stripped and hanged upside down by her ankles. She was then doused with gasoline and motor oil. Her stomach was split open with a knife; her innocent, helpless unborn baby fell to the ground and was stomped and crushed to death. The woman was then set on fire while still alive and then riddled with hundreds of bullets by the angry mob. And to think, some called the Native Americans savages. What could be more savage than this? This type of public savagery and brutality was designed to keep certain people in line.

The brutal and savage lynching and murder of Mack Charles Parker also gathered national attention on the way the law enforcement, police, and church leaders worked together to lynch and murder people that stepped out of line and didn't follow their code.

In 1959 Mack Charles Parker was arrested for the alleged rape of a White woman in Poplarville, Mississippi. One of the Mississippi state troopers that had arrested Mr. Parker offered his service revolver to the woman's husband to shoot him on the spot. The husband refused because his wife said she was not sure that Mr. Parker had been the one who had raped her.

After Mr. Parker was jailed, a former deputy sheriff went to a prayer meeting and recruited a lynch mob led by a Baptist minister. Mr. Parker was dragged from his cell aided by the jailer and murdered, and his body was thrown in the Pearl River. Most of the murderers were identified, but the state of Mississippi refused to prosecute anyone for Mr. Parker's murder.

Many White Good Samaritans Were Also Victims of Violent Racism

African Americans were not and have not always been the only target for racial violent hate groups. Many caring and concerned Good Samaritan White people, especially Christians throughout history who wanted to assist in the struggle for justice and equality for all of God's children, were also harassed, beaten, jailed, and even murdered by hate groups who maliciously took the position that God created and ordained them superior and to be in control. This is not a mandate of God but of Satan.

Shortly after the signing of the Emancipation Proclamation and enactment on January 1, 1863, hate groups mobilized to thwart equality that was trying to be done through the Republican Party and others. The Emancipation Proclamation was to abolish slavery, but former slaves still needed legislation passed to provide for citizenship and voting rights.

The Republican Party was able to get the Thirteenth, Fourteenth, and Fifteenth Amendment passed over the opposition of the Democratic Party and other racial hate groups. The Republican Party was also able to get a number of Black and former slaves elected to public office. This did not sit well with the Democratic Party, so they helped form hate groups such as the Ku Klux Klan to terrorize, lynch, and murder Blacks as well as Whites that supported Blacks.

Between 1863 and 1962 there were over forty-eight hundred lynchings recorded in the United States. One out of four was a White person. Whites who were trying to assist in the struggle for justice would be lynched just like a Black person.

Lynchings were a very cruel, savage, barbaric, and inhumane way to kill someone. They were done publicly so they would send a message to others. Many Whites that tried to aid in seeking equality for all faced the same violence from hate groups, as did the Blacks.

Harriet Tubman's Underground Railroad would not have been nearly as successful if it had not been for some of her White supporters. These Whites put their lives and the lives of their family in danger, and some were killed for supporting the Underground Railroad. Most of the weigh stations that provided refuge and a hiding place for runaway slaves were owned by sympathetic Whites.

Dr. Martin L. King Jr. was supported by many White clergy and White citizens who subjected themselves and their families to unthinkable danger by supporting him. Many more were actually killed for their efforts. Most of the Freedom Riders that made such an impact on the civil rights struggle were young White college students from the North. Many of these Freedom Riders endured unthinkable suffering and even death for their efforts.

There were many other good Samaritan Whites who paid the supreme sacrifice for the cause of justice and equality, not including the 640,000 to 700,000 men who died during the Civil War. Just as the history writers failed to record the many contributions of African Americans, they also failed to record the contributions of many of the Whites that gave their lives for the cause of civil rights.

These Good Samaritans, mostly Christian White people, didn't just give free labor for the cause; they gave in many cases the supreme sacrifice of their lives. Their heirs just like the heirs of former slaves have not inherited because of their family's sacrifice. Should their White heirs also be entitled to reparations for their heir's contribution?

What about the five small children Viola Liuzzo left behind without a mother when she was murdered trying to help secure the rights for African Americans? What about all the other White children that had to grow up without a parent to support them because that parent was killed trying to help secure the rights for African Americans? Is there really a fair way to determine reparations when we take into consideration the sacrifices so many non-African Americans have also made?

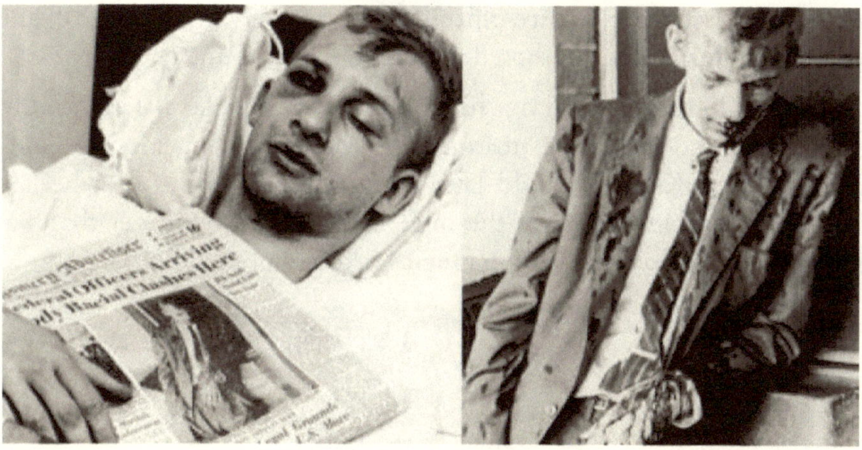

James Zwerg

Freedom Rider *James Zwerg* was brutally and savagely beaten in Jackson, Mississippi, by a racist White mob in 1962 while the Jackson, Mississippi, police stood by and did nothing to protect him or other Freedom Riders that had come to Mississippi and other Southern cities to protest the racial injustice that existed at the time.

Most Freedom Riders were met with hostility, hatred, physical attacks, and even death; but they still continued to come and support the cause. The Freedom Riders made one of the most important impacts on the cause for justice. It was the Freedom Riders that brought national attention to the shameful and disgraceful way America treated its citizens of Color.

Rev. Bruce Klunder

Rev. Bruce Klunder was only an eighteen years old college student in Oregon but was so moved by the injustice he saw during the Montgomery Boycott until he helped raise money to support the movement. Rev. Klunder, like so many others around the world, stood in total shock and disbelief to actually witness women and small children trampled by horses being ridden by police officers, being beaten with billy clubs, and tear gassed during the attempted march on Bloody Sunday.

Rev. Klunder stepped out his comfort zone to take a stand against such savage and inhumane treatment he witnessed happening to God's children. Rev. Klunder would later be crushed to death when he laid his body down in protest in the mud in front of a bulldozer that was attempting to break ground for a segregated school in 1964.

William Moore

William Moore stepped outside his comfort zone many times and had a long history of protesting segregation. He had been arrested for protesting segregation many times during his life. He had been arrested for protesting segregated movie theaters and other businesses that discriminated against Black citizens. He was best-known for his walking long distances to deliver messages against segregation. William Moore once walked from Baltimore to the state capitol and again to Washington, DC, to deliver a letter to President Kennedy. He was walking from Chattanooga in April 1963, but shortly after crossing the Alabama state line, William Moore was gunned down like a mad stray dog.

Rev. James Reeb

In 1965 *Rev. James Reeb* already had a reputation in the Washington, DC, area for being willing to step outside his comfort zone to aid those in need. When he heard the call from Dr. King for help in Selma, he boarded a plane against the advice of his wife and others. One night in Selma, after he and several ministers were trying to find their way, they came in contact with an angry racist White mob. The mob attacked them with heavy clubs. Rev. Reeb was hit in the head by one of the angry White men. One in the mob said, "Now you know what it feels like to be a nigger in Alabama." The hospital refused to treat him until they could raise the medical fees. By the time the medical fees were raised and Rev. Reeb was taken to the hospital, it was too late. Rev. Reeb died from his injuries.

Viola Gregg Liuzzo

In 1965 Viola Liuzzo, a young thirty-nine-year-old mother of five children, left Michigan to assist with the Selma March after Bloody Sunday. Mrs. Liuzzo was helping transport marchers between Selma and Montgomery. On one of her trips, Mrs. Liuzzo noticed a carload of Klansmen following her. She tried to get away from them by accelerating her speed. The Klansmen following her continued accelerating to speeds of over one hundred miles per hour. The Klansmen's car pulled up beside Mrs. Liuzzo's car and fired two shots through her window. The bullets shattered Mrs. Liuzzo's skull. LeRoy Moton, her Black passenger, tried to take control of the car, but the car crashed into an embankment. The Klansmen then came up to the car, shining their flashlights, making sure their bullets had found their mark and the job had been done. Moton lay still and pretended to be dead. Mrs. Liuzzo was dead from her gunshot wounds.

Jonathan Daniels

Jonathan Daniels was a twenty-six-year old student at Episcopal Seminary in Cambridge, Massachusetts, when he decided to step outside his comfort zone and answer the nationwide call from Dr. Martin L. King Jr. for all clergy to come to the aid of the people in need in Selma, Alabama. Daniels answered the call and went to Selma. He and others were boycotting some businesses that segregated against Blacks when they were all arrested and kept in jail for over a week. They were then released without any transportation or direction. Daniels and one of his companions went to a local store but were met by a deputy sheriff with a shotgun who told them to leave or he would shoot them. The deputy sheriff fired his shotgun, killing Daniels and wounding his companion.

The deputy was tried in front of an all-White jury that voted not guilty, as had been done in so many other cases where an all-White jury would vote not guilty in cases where a white person had murdered a

Black person or a White person who was trying to aid a Black person in such a case of justice.

These Whites that decided to step outside their comfort zone to aid in the cause of humanity and human rights were in many cases labeled as "Nigger lovers." I guess they were in good company because Jesus would have also been called a Nigger lover. For not only did he love us all, he created us all and gave up his life as a living sacrifice for us all.

When we hate a person because of their race, we are in fact telling God we disagree with what he has created. So racism is not a social issue; it is a spiritual issue. Racism is an attempt to disagree with God. No one can be a racist and say they love God, for it is a contradiction (1 John 4:20).

Ambush on Martinsville Road

After I signed up to integrate and attend Mendenhall High in 1965, things became even more dangerous for my family. The people that were opposed to a Black child receiving an education with White children became very upset with my decision to integrate the all-White Mendenhall High School. There were a lot of threats as well as attempts to assault, injure, and even kill.

One day prior to the semester I was scheduled to integrate Mendenhall High School, my younger brother Dwight and I were shot at by some young White male teenagers while we were walking home from our uncle's house. My uncle's house was about a quarter of a mile or so from our house.

Dwight and I had stopped along the side of the country road on the way home to pick some wild plums. I suddenly heard something singing through the plum tree branches. I looked back and saw two White boys shooting at us. Dwight and I ran home, got my daddy's single-shot shotgun, and the boys that had been shooting at us ran like frightened rabbits.

We knew who these boys were. They were our neighbors who lived down the road from us. We were afraid to tell my dad what had happened because we knew he would try to do something about it, which would have probably gotten my dad in trouble. We did not report it to the police because it was well understood nothing would be done to a White person for shooting at a Black person or even killing a Black person in Mississippi during those days.

My dad did find out about the incident a few weeks later. He was very upset we had not told him about it. My dad went to the parents of the boys that had shot at us, and the father of the boys said he would punish them for what they had done. Their punishment ended up being losing the privilege to ride their bicycles for one week. I guess that's how much Black lives mattered in Mississippi.

Then, one day I was walking home from school because I had missed the bus. We lived about four miles from the school. My dad had a policy that if you missed the bus, you had better somehow beat the bus home. As I was running down that old Martinsville Country Road trying to beat the bus home, a pickup truck pulled up behind me. All I heard was, "That's that Nigger."

The next thing I saw was one of the White guys on the back of the pickup truck throw a large piece of metal at my head. It was a very close call, because if that piece of metal had hit me in the head, it would have surely killed me. I was able to cut through the woods to elude them. I was still able to beat the bus home because I was more fearful of violating my dad's rules than that of some sick racist White boys.

A few weeks later, I, along with several young Black members of our local church, was walking home after vacation Bible school when we were ambushed and shot at by a group of White radicals. We had just left Bible study and wanted to walk home from church.

The church was about one mile from our house on Martinsville Road. My dad had warned us that it might be dangerous walking home because of the many threats we had received. There were several dark spots between the church and our house. Country roads had no streetlights, and with no moon shining, it could get very dark on one of those Mississippi country roads. We wanted to walk because we would get the chance to walk with some girls that lived about halfway between our house and the church.

Shortly after walking the girl's home, we were approaching my granddad's farm, which was about a quarter of a mile from our house. It was a very dark spot in the road because these were farmhouses, and most farmhouses were at least a quarter of a mile apart in the country. So the only light might come from a farmhouse because there were no streets lights in the country.

It was my brothers Steadman Jr., Paul, and Dwight, my cousins Donald, Tim, Randy, Dexter, and me. We could barely see the pickup truck that was parked in the darkness on the side of the road in between the two farmhouses waiting to ambush us as we approached.

It was so dark that we could not make out the pickup truck until we were right up on it. I remember one of my cousins saying, after seeing a dark object on the side of the road just a few yards in front of us, "What's that?" At that same moment, some White guys that had been waiting in the darkness to ambush us turned the headlights on in the pickup truck, and one had a spotlight that he shined on us as we ran for cover across my granddad's pasture. Another said, "Get those Niggers." We then heard a shotgun blast several times in our direction as one of the guys shined a spotlight on us.

We were able to escape by ducking and running through my granddad's cow pasture. One cousin, Dexter, was not quite as familiar with the layout of our granddad's pasture as the rest of us. Dexter did not know about the smaller pasture within the bigger pasture.

My granddad had a smaller fenced-in pasture within the bigger pasture to keep smaller cattle. This was so that they would not get lost or attacked by some of the wild animals like wolves, panthers, and bobcats that were known to attack smaller cattle in the big pasture that extended for several miles from my granddad's house. We were all familiar with this except for Dexter, who didn't know about the smaller pasture within the bigger pasture. We all knew to fall and roll under the fence when we ran to the smaller pasture.

It was so dark, and Dexter didn't know and couldn't see the fence of the smaller pasture. He ran into our granddad's fence of the smaller pasture, which was the calf's pasture, and took out about twenty fence posts, pulling them completely out of the ground, but Dexter never lost stride. We still laugh about that even today how Dexter took out about twenty of our granddad's fence posts but never lost his stride and was able to beat the rest of us to our grandfather's house while crawling on his knees and hands.

The fence knocked him down, but he was able to crawl as fast on all four as we were standing up and running. Dexter later joked and told us after we were safe and out of danger that after the fence knocked him down, he just shifted into four-wheel drive.

The Voting Rights Act

Segregated public accommodations were not the only problems that African Americans had to deal with at the time. Most African Americans were denied the right to vote. The right to vote could bring about some major changes for the state of Mississippi and other Southern states because in many cities in the South, African Americans made up the majority of the population.

I was recently a candidate for the city council in the City of Dallas, Texas. The district that I was running out of has over forty thousand voters. A candidate can win a seat on the council in my district with less than two thousand votes. This is a disgrace and a shame!

There were so many efforts made by the Jim Crow followers to deny African-Americans the right to vote. After the country decided to make it unlawful to deny the African American the right to vote, there were so many other schemes designed to prevent the African American from voting.

Some states imposed a poll tax. This tax was a direct attempt to prevent the African Americans from voting. Then there was the literacy test, which was in most cases only required of the African American voter. When these two efforts failed, Mr. Crow would discourage the African American from voting by making sure the employer kept the African American on the job during the voting time.

There was also, in many cases, a list kept of all African Americans that voted. This was easily accomplished because there was generally only one voting place. This one voting place was usually at the courthouse where all could see. Many African Americans that voted would lose their job because they had exercised their right to vote.

During my campaign for the Dallas city council, I walked and canvassed my district trying to get out the vote in the African American community. I came across this one African American gentleman who was sitting on his front porch drinking a beer in the middle of a workday, which meant he probably didn't have a job. I asked him if he were going to vote. He replied, "For what?"

I made my best attempt to explain to him the sacrifices my dad and so many others had made for him to just have the right to vote. He then asked me where and when could he vote. I told him we have made it so easy now to vote. There will be two whole weeks of early voting and then the polls would be opened from 7:00 a.m. until 7:00 p.m. on Election Day. I told him his voting place was within walking distance directly across the street from him. He told me he would think about it. I thought, "What a shame and disgrace."

It is a bigger shame to know and understand the supreme sacrifice some made for the right to vote and how some of us who will vote sell our vote so cheaply. Some don't vote and many vote for all the wrong reasons or persons. In many cases, it does not matter about experience or qualification. It matters more about party affiliation or in some cases, what race, gender, or sexual orientation the candidate is.

It is an embarrassment and a shame how African Americans have been misled politically and religiously. Many politicians are not held accountable when it comes to the African American vote. They get the African American vote and their African American voter seldom see or hear from them again until it's time to vote.

In many cases, the candidate is not qualified and has no experience or concern in dealing with African American issues, but African Americans will blindly and ignorantly vote for them anyway.

I had the privilege of serving as a Texas precinct chairman/judge for about twenty years. During my tenure, I discovered voting unintelligently and blindly was not limited to African Americans. I discovered far too many voters vote for the wrong person and the wrong reason.

Many Democrats vote for Democrats no matter what their qualifications or views. Many Republicans will likewise vote for a Republican even if the Republican is diametrically in opposition to their political views. Women will in many cases vote for a woman simply because she is a woman. Blacks will often vote for another Black just because he/she is Black. Lesbian, gay, bisexual, and transgender (LGBT) will generally vote for a candidate that identifies with their group.

I was somewhat encouraged when my daughter Sabrina stated she understood what her grandfather Steadman Hays and others had gone through just so she would have the right to vote, and she would never miss the opportunity to vote and would never vote for any candidate that did not support her political views. Thanks, Dad. Your granddaughter is proof your sacrifice was not totally in vain.

I have tried, like my father, to impress upon and pass on to my children the importance of voting, being involved, and taking a position on issues that are important to them, their family, and their community. I have tried to impress upon them to be independent thinkers and not to vote for or support anyone just because of their race, gender, or political party.

I believe at least one of my children got the message, because even though I was a state delegate for George W. Bush, a Republican presidential candidate, which caused me to have to go against the popular opinion that African Americans are supposed to support Democrats and not Republicans, my daughter Sabrina was a senatorial delegate for Barack Obama, a Democratic presidential candidate, which also caused her to have to go against the popular opinion that women are supposed to support a woman and not a man when opposed by a woman.

It is also true with religion. Many African Americans as well as other churchgoing people don't read the Bible enough for themselves. They are therefore left open for any doctrine that comes out of the mouths of many false prophets the Bible warned us about (Matt. 7:15–20). Many will just follow like lost sheep any and all commands they are given. This is one of the reasons there is so much abuse in the church today, because people will just follow blindly like lost sheep. These issues will be discussed in more detail in a later chapter.

How Integration May Have Damaged African Americans

Years have passed, civil rights, voting rights, and integration have occurred. But what effect has all this had on the American society? I was first confused by a statement made by one of my heroes, James Meredith, who in 1962 had become my hero when he was courageous enough to step outside his comfort zone and integrate the University of Mississippi. I stood with so much pride on that cool afternoon in September 1962 when I witnessed as a junior high school student my hero, James Meredith, being escorted by US Marshals on to the campus of Mississippi State University.

James Meredith had served in the military but could not attend the only law school in his home state of Mississippi. There had been no other Black person that had been allowed to attend the University of Mississippi even though it was the only law school in the state.

Years later Mr. Meredith would make the statement that puzzled me. The statement was, "The worst thing that had ever happened to Black People in America was integration and welfare." I didn't understand. He had become my hero, had risked his life, several people had been killed and many injured because he integrated Mississippi State University. I had put my family in danger by following after him when I signed up to integrate Mendenhall High School. Was he now saying it was a mistake?

I had always thought integration and welfare were good for the country because integration would promote equality and welfare was instituted to help people meet basic human needs. There was a lot of disparity and poverty in Mississippi as well as many other places.

Integration and welfare were one way a lot of these people would be able to meet their basic human needs. Many of these people, because of racism, in many cases were Black people. How could Mr. Meredith now say welfare and integration were bad for Blacks?

Segregated While Integrated

After analyzing all that happened during the so-called integration of most schools in many places, one may agree with Mr. Meredith. My high school in particular had been founded by Rev. C. H. Harper, a Black minister. Rev. Harper had founded Harper Vocational School in order to help prepare Black people in Mississippi for the changing society.

Most Blacks in Mississippi during Rev. Harper's day had very little education and few job skills other than farming. The Industrial Revolution was changing the way people farmed and the whole work industry. This change would mean there would be a lot of Blacks unemployed with no skills to keep up with the changing times. Rev. Harper's vision was to educate and help acquire skills for Blacks in Mississippi to become more marketable when these changes came.

The Simpson County Board of Education later funded the school and adopted it as the only public school for Blacks in Mendenhall, Mississippi. Surprisingly, the school was allowed to keep its founder's name, Harper. It was not much of a school, but it was all Black people had in Mendenhall, Mississippi, and we were proud of it.

One shabby building housed the elementary, junior high, and high school. There were few educational tools and a few books that were used, hand-me-downs from the White Mendenhall schools.

The library had one used set of World Book Encyclopedia, one dictionary, and probably less than fifty other books. The building did not have indoor plumbing, and of course, it did not have air-conditioning. But the Black students didn't need air-conditioning anyway, because most of the Black students were the children of sharecroppers. They were therefore not allowed to attend school until the crops were harvested generally in November.

It was not very much of a school, but Blacks in Mendenhall, Mississippi, were very proud of their school. Many Black men would come in on their own time to make repairs, paint, and do whatever necessary to make the school better. Many Black women would also volunteer their time to help by cleaning and assisting in preparing lunch for the students.

The Simpson County Board of Education voted to start the White schools in September, but the Black school would not start a regular school year until the end of October. From September to the end of October, the Black school would only operate a half a day so that the Black students could get out of school at noon to join their parents working in the fields. Many of these Black students didn't even enroll in school until after the crops were harvested in November or December.

In 1960, with the passage of the freedom of choice legislation meant students should have the right to attend the school of their choice in their district, the Simpson County School Board decided to build a brand-new school for Black students. It was a new modern school, which was actually newer and looked better than the White school. This was to keep any Black student from wanting to attend the White school.

We were so proud of our new Harper Vocational High School. My older sister Evelyn was a senior and was in the first class to graduate from the new school. There was a tradition at Harper High to have each graduating class picture displayed in the main hallway of the building. I was so proud, impressed, and inspired each time I passed down that hall by that picture and saw my sister Evelyn distinguished as the president of her graduating class.

Three years later, my brother Steadman "Pete" Hays Jr.'s class graduated. Pete was not distinguished by being president of his class; as a matter of fact, if it had not been for the grace of God and the fear of the wrath of my dad, Pete probably would not have made the Hall of Fame. But he did and we were proud of each class that made that wall very special because it represented probably the most important recorded history for Black people in Mendenhall, Mississippi.

My year finally came, and my class picture was displayed on the wall. A few years later, my brother Dwight's class, and few years after that my brother Michael made the wall.

My family was well represented in the history of the school. My dad had attended the school, and his sister Martha was in the first class to graduate. There were many of my cousins and friends that also attended Harper High. Most Blacks in Mendenhall had either attended Harper High or had a family member that did. Whenever we visited the school, that wall was the main attraction.

Then! Integration.

When the schools finally integrated, Harper High was turned into Mendenhall Junior High School. There was no surprise to most disappointed Black people in Mendenhall when this happened, and the Harper High history went down with the Harper High sign. But this was not the most shameful thing that happened. My younger sister Cynthia and my younger brother Gregory would never see their pictures displayed on the walls of Harper High, as did their older brothers and sister.

A few years after integration and the downfall of Harper High, I was visiting my hometown church. I was strolling through the Fellowship Hall when I noticed the pictures that had once been the main attraction of Harper High hall hung on the walls of the Fellowship Hall of my hometown church.

I inquired why the pictures that meant so much to Black people in Mendenhall were in the Fellowship Hall of my hometown church. I was told they were found in the trash bins behind the school by one of the school's custodians who just happened to be a member of my hometown church.

According to the custodian, the pictures were removed from the school and thrown in the trash bins by some White teachers and administrators when the White children entered the school. This was such a shameful display of racism, disrespect, and hatred.

They could have just called any Black parent or Black citizen that would have been more than happy and proud to have removed the pictures and taken them to a place of honor rather than disrespectfully and disgracefully throwing them in the trash as has been done with a lot of Black history in this country after integration.

My younger brother Gregory and my younger sister Cynthia ended up going to the new integrated Mendenhall schools. According to some, integration was not really integration. They were integrated but still segregated. They were in the same school with the White students, but the White students were placed in sections A and B, while the Black students were placed in sections C and D.

Mr. Meredith, I think I finally see your point about integration was in some ways bad for Black people. While the segregated Black schools may have been poor in resources, they were rich in pride and history. Much of that pride and rich history was destroyed with integration. Just as integration destroyed the rich history of Rev. C. H. Harper High School, many other Black historians and Black institutions met the same fate.

Prior to integration, almost every major city in America had a Booker T. Washington, a George Washington Carver, a Franklin Delano Roosevelt, and a Lincoln black school. Few of those historical Black schools exist today because of integration. Just as my high school, Harper High's history was thrown in the trash bins of history when integration occurred, so were most of those Black schools' history were also thrown into America's historical trash bins.

I now understand why Mr. Meredith would have made such a statement about integration, but I was still struggling with the statement concerning welfare. Before welfare Black families were one of the most cohesive family units in America. Black men worked hard at any job they could get to support their family. The Black family valued their biblical vows "until death do us part" very seriously.

Today more than 50 percent of Black families in America are headed by single parents. What has happened to the Black family in America?

One major problem is not welfare as my hero James Meredith and some will say, but I say it is the misuse of welfare and the way it has been implemented.

A lot of welfare women today have decided to shack up and live with a man rather than marry and live as a family because marriage would affect their ability to get welfare. So, the misuse of the welfare system can be partly responsible for so many single-parent homes today.

To some, welfare has become an addictive lifestyle. I have witnessed this addiction firsthand pass from grandmother, to daughter, to granddaughter. It's a dependency on a handout that causes a person to lose any ambition and desire to do for themselves. Take away a man's ambition and that man becomes a parasite with no hope. Welfare has been part of the hopelessness of a many of people.

So, Mr. Meredith, I now also understand your statement about welfare. Welfare has caused so many families to lose hope and is now passing that hopelessness generationally to children, grandchildren, and no one knows where it may end. Mr. Meredith, I now understand better what you meant.

When I see so many healthy people standing on the street corners, homeless, begging for handouts rather than trying to get a job, I understand much better what damage the welfare system has done. It goes back to the Confucius saying, "Give a man a fish and he will have food for a day; teach a man to fish and he will have food forever." I say, "Give a man a fish and he will expect you to give him one tomorrow; give him a job and make him earn that fish and he will know he must earn that fish tomorrow." I thank God my dad never allowed us to accept government handouts and be on welfare. None of Steadman Hays's, my dad's, eight children have ever been on welfare.

If welfare causes so much complacency and destroys the motivation and incentive to work and provide a living for oneself, I can only image what reparations could do. Would reparations cause another generation to become complacent and dependent on a governmental handout?

Reparation

I also don't support the movement for reparation for the heirs of former slaves if the results will be like the dysfunctional welfare system and lead to another crisis of expectation of another governmental handout that would cause some to expect something that they didn't directly work for or earn. I know this will not be a popular position for an African American who most certainly can and has traced his family history through some of the turbulent years of slavery and can show even today some of the aftermath effects slavery has caused to his family to take such a position.

I am however bold enough to step outside my comfort zone and speak what I believe to be the truth and not what is necessarily considered politically correct. I cannot support any movement that may cause a generation of people to become apathetic and give up hope because of an expectation of a governmental handout rather than getting a job and trying to be self-sufficient.

I do understand and do however disagree with the argument that some heirs of former White slave owners make that they did not enslave anyone and should not have to pay for the sins of their father. I agree that they should not have to pay for the sins of their father, but I do believe following that same argument; they should not likewise be allowed to benefit from the sins of their father either.

Many White heirs of former White slave owners in America today are enjoying the benefits in the form of inheritances of their heirs free slave labor even today while many African American heirs of former slaves are still suffering from not being able to inherit from their heirs because their heirs were forced to work for free and therefore had nothing to pass down by way of inheritance.

Each time I drive down Martinsville Road in Simpson County, Mississippi, my hometown today, and see the White families owning and living on land that my ancestors worked, developed for free from slave labor, I am reminded of how Whites are still benefiting even today from slave labor.

So, what is the answer? For me, I will let God have the last say and deal with this most difficult issue. Because if we try to correct all the wrongs by reparations that man has imposed, the White European male will probably be making reparations to almost everyone that he has dealt with in America.

If we consider everyone who has been mistreated and discriminated against by the White male in America, reparations would probably be expected to more than just African Americans. I do understand and agree that the African American has been the only group of people in America that has been enslaved and forced to work for free; but women, the Native American, the Chinese American, the Mexican American, the Jewish American, and so on have all been discriminated, exploited, and not paid the same as the white Male in America. Should they be paid reparations too?

In the last few years there has been a lot of political rhetoric and talk by politicians about reparation. I believe that is all it is—political talk in an attempt to maybe get some uninformed person to vote for them. For there is no logical or equitable way reparations could be equitably and fairly distributed.

Some have suggested forty acres and a mule. Some have suggested that all White heirs of former slave owners should be required to pay a reparation tax to benefit heirs of African American slaves. Some have suggested reducing taxes for heirs of African American slaves.

The problem with all these suggestions is, there is no just way to determine who actually suffered and who benefited and to what degree from slavery. Just as all Whites did not directly benefit from slavery, not all African Americans directly suffered from slavery.

So I would again suggest that some things we learn from our past and we allow God to have the last say and be the final just judge of our deeds and move on to some real issues, like "Can we just get along?"

My dad didn't believe in welfare or reparations and taught his children to earn their living by getting a good education and working hard. He did not allow his children to make or accept excuses regardless of the difficulty of the situation, just as he would not allow me to make any excuses for not going to law school.

He insisted on me going to law school even though my vocational high school had not prepared me for college and not to mention law school or the fact that there were no law schools in my home state, the state of Mississippi, that would admit African Americans at the time.

"You Are the One"

After finishing high school, I had to decide the next step for my career. My dad had always encouraged all his children to attend college and had always encouraged me to also attend law school and become an attorney so that he and so many other people who had not had access to the legal system could now have access.

I had no idea how my dad thought I could attend law school and become an attorney. I had never even seen or met an attorney except Perry Mason on a television show. Mississippi only had one law school, which was segregated, and Blacks were not allowed to attend the only law school in the state of Mississippi, the University of Mississippi.

Mississippi was the poorest state in the Union with the worst educational system in the country. This was where I had been educated. It was difficult for the White students from Mississippi to be competitive locally and nationally, but it was more traumatic for the Black students. The Mississippi White citizens had all the money and all the power. The state was totally segregated with the White citizens in control.

Most Black citizens had to be sharecroppers where the crops never brought in enough money to get out of debt. It was a form of legalized slavery because they were enslaved and had to continue working for the landowner until a never-ending debt was paid. This was one of the reasons my grandfather always wanted to own his own land. Land ownership meant freedom. Most other Blacks that were not sharecroppers worked on jobs where they were paid just enough to get by and avoid starvation.

I guess my family was more fortunate than most Black families in Mississippi at that time. My grandfather's father, Washington Hays Jr. had gone to President William McKinley and had been awarded a land grant. He had been granted a large amount of land to farm and maintain for a certain number of years, and then the land would be deeded over to him.

Most of that land remained in the Hays family until the late 1950s when a White neighbor tricked my grandfather Walter Hays into signing a warranty deed thinking he was signing a one-year lease. My dad was devastated when he found out what had happened. Most of that land was part of the land grant that was granted to Washington Hays Jr., my grandfather's father.

In 1862 there had been legislation passed that allowed a person to petition the government for a certain amount of land to farm. If the person receiving the land grant successfully farmed the land for a certain number of years, he could then petition the government for a deed.

This was how my grandfather's father Washington Hays Jr. was able to secure a deed that bears the presidential seal and the signature of President William McKinley. The document was dated and executed one month before President McKinley was assassinated. I proudly display a copy of the original document hanging in my law office today.

My dad did everything he could within the legal system to correct the injustice that had been done by our White neighbor who had stolen my grandfather's land. But the legal system of justice did not apply to Black people in Mississippi in those days.

There were no Black attorneys in Simpson County, Mississippi, and no White attorney would dare represent a Black citizen against a White citizen. My dad and his family, as did most Black citizens, had to accept the harsh reality that Black citizens had no legal rights and no access to the legal system in the state of Mississippi.

My dad used this horrible disgraceful experience to influence one of his six boys to go to law school so that there might be hope for people who had no hope within the legal system of Mississippi. I will never forget when my dad told me, "Son, you need to study hard and go to college and then to law school so that others will have the help we did not receive." "Dad, what are you talking about?"

The reason this was such a phenomenal request was because the state of Mississippi, my home state, had only one law school and that school did not allow Blacks to attend. The other reason this request was so phenomenal was we had no money and I was not being prepared for college in my vocational high school, let alone law school.

Mississippi had the poorest educational system in the country, and the Black students were worse off than the White students because of the Jim Crow laws, the so-called separate but equal system, which had taken its toll on most Black students. Most Black students in Mississippi were not prepared for college in the Mississippi Black schools.

Mississippi couldn't afford one educational system but was trying to operate two separate ones. This attempt to try to run two separate school systems did much harm and damage to the White students and even more harm and damage to the African American students because the African American students got the hand-me-downs from the White schools.

In this so-called separate but equal system, the Black students received the hand-me-down textbooks, run-down schools and modes of transportation. To make matters worse, the Black high school was a vocational school that was created to teach vocational training and not college preparatory.

To make matters more difficult, the White schools started their school year at the beginning of September. The Black school did not start their full day of classes until the end of October. Since most Black families were sharecroppers, most Black students could not attend school until after the crops were harvested.

The Black schools would only open for a half a day until after October, which meant, not only did the White children have better schools, books, and transportation, they also went to school almost twice the time Black children did.

This however was not taken into consideration when the Black students had to compete. The Black children had to take and pass the same curriculum as did the White children. The Black students had to pass the same college entrance exam. That's why I can't understand why some today are so opposed and don't understand what affirmative action was attempting to correct.

I will never forget what my dad's words were when I told him that I was not being prepared to go to college at my vocational school and that there were no law schools in the state of Mississippi that accepted Black students, and even if they did, we had no money.

I told my dad that only one in ten thousand in my situation would even think of going to law school. I'll never forget my dad's response. He said, "Son, you are looking at the wrong number. You are looking at the ten thousand, son. *You are the one.*" My dad went on to give me a lecture on how we should not focus on the problem but should focus on the one who can solve the problem. He said, "David would not have been successful against the giant had he focused on the giant, but David was successful because he focused on the one that could bring the giant down.'

I tried to explain to my dad that we were in Mississippi and Mississippi had not prepared his son to go to college. I could almost hear my dad's wisdom as if he were saying, "It's not the place that defines you. It's what you do while in the place that defines you." I knew this was the wisdom of my dad because of an incident and a sermon he had once preached.

My dad had been one of the most outspoken opponents against nightclubs and places that sold alcohol in our small hometown. He had lived and seen the devastation of alcohol abuse, having grown up with an alcoholic father. My oldest brother, Pete, who generally defied and challenged most of my dad's rules, didn't agree with him. Pete often frequented nightclubs and places that sold alcohol. Pete was also known to sometimes consume alcohol, which did not meet approval with our father.

On this one night, someone that did not like my dad's relentless attacks on nightclubs decided to play a dirty trick on him. They called my dad's house in the middle of the night and told him his son Pete had been killed at this nightclub. This of course was not true, but my dad didn't know it at the time.

My dad got up and drove over to the nightclub, only to find out that it was only a dirty trick. The following week the news spread like wildfire that the outspoken Rev. Steadman Hays, who was always speaking out against nightclubs, had been seen at one.

I will never forget how my dad handled the situation and what he had to say in his sermon the following Sunday morning. The church was packed with people to see what Rev. Hays would have to say about what the community was spreading about him attending a nightclub. There were more people in church that Sunday than most Sundays.

My dad's scripture reading came from 1 John 2:15–17, "In the world but not of the world." He concluded his sermon by saying, "It is true I visited a nightclub, but my presence in the nightclub didn't pull my status down. My presence in the nightclub pulled the status of the nightclub up." Preach on, Rev. Hays.

After remembering my dad's sermon and his words of wisdom on how we should not let a place define us, I realized I was letting my home state, Mississippi, define me. Mississippi had defined me as well as most of its Black citizens as being suited only as farmers and common laborers and not for college and professional careers.

It was true; my home state, Mississippi, had failed to adequately educate and prepare me for anything other than as a farmer or a common laborer, but was I going to let my home state, Mississippi, define me, or was I going to follow my dad's advice and only let God, who had created me unique for a special purpose, define me? My dad reminded me of a saying: "If the sky was meant to be the limits, what was heaven made for?"

The Lower You Are, the Higher You Can Climb
College

After finishing my vocational high school training, I decided with the constant encouragement of my father to step outside my comfort zone and accept my dad's challenge to go to college and then to law school. I knew it would not be easy, and later, there were many times during my career that I felt overwhelmed and wanted to quit, but I would hear my dad's voice saying, "Son, *you are the one*."

I remember leaving Mississippi to accept a scholarship at a college in Dallas, Texas. There were students from all over the world we would have to compete with. There were eight of my fellow classmates that left Mississippi with me to attend Bishop College in Dallas, Texas. It would be a big challenge to leave a small town in Mississippi and compete with students from all over the world.

We were required to pass an English proficiency test to enter college in the fall. I remember arriving in the big city and feeling so inadequate and unprepared. When my test results returned, I was devastated. I had graduated from my vocational high school with honors, but I scored on an eighth-grade level on the National English Proficiency Test.

All my Mississippi classmates didn't do any better. This score meant we were not prepared or ready for college. Our state, Mississippi, and our school system had failed and not prepared us for college. We never realized just how much damage the Jim Crow system had done to us.

All my classmates, except for one, gave up, accepted defeat, and returned to Mississippi. I felt like doing the same, but I could hear my dad's voice saying, "Son, you are the one." My dad's voice and the fact that I had nothing to return to Mississippi for were enough motivation for me to be willing to do anything to succeed.

The school had a three-month college preparatory summer program for students who were not ready for college. I registered for the program and was assigned a sponsor. My sponsor was a White male professor. It was very difficult for me at first to relate to a White person on a personal basis after having gone through what most Blacks had experienced growing up in Mississippi.

Most Whites I had experienced in Mississippi did not want a Black person to succeed because this would cause the professional Black person to reject being treated like a second-class citizen. This was not good for the status quo in Mississippi.

I soon realized I was totally wrong about my views on most Whites. I had to realize that most White people were not like what I had experienced in Mississippi. My sponsor could relate to discrimination and the damage it could cause. He was very sympathetic and understanding of what Blacks had experienced in the segregated Jim Crow South and was very supportive. He understood the need for affirmative action and was almost as encouraging as my dad.

He did everything possible to encourage and assist me with my many academic deficiencies. He would even come over to my dormitory after class to make sure I was able to keep up. He tutored me at night, on weekends, and whenever necessary, sometimes on his own off time to make sure I was ready for college in the fall. He would later encourage and assist me getting a fellowship to one of the most prestigious law schools in the country.

After an intense three-month enrichment program, I was scheduled to retake the college entrance exam. This was the same exam I had just three months earlier scored on an eighth-grade level. The enrichment program, the tutoring, and the encouragement from my sponsor had paid off. I had scored the highest improvement of all the students in the program.

This situation reminded me of what my dad had once told me: "If you trust in God, God will never put you in a situation without providing resources to assist you." With the help of my sponsor, I had gone from an eighth-grade level to a sophomore in college level in just three months.

This situation also reminded me of another principle my dad had always tried to instill in his children about giving up. "Just because you start at the bottom is no reason to give up. For the lower you are, the higher you can climb." I started as the lowest but had finished the highest.

I would like to say everything went well after that and everyone lived happily ever after. But the deficiencies of my formal education continued to create issues for me. And the original eight students from my class was now down to one—me. The last one gave up and moved back to Mississippi too.

I was however able to struggle through college while working full-time at night to support myself. It was a difficult struggle, but each time the thought crossed my mind to give up, I could hear my dad's voice saying, "You are the one." In the end, I can testify it was well worth it.

Law School

After finishing college, I applied and was accepted at one of the top African American law schools in the country, the prestigious Howard University in Washington, DC. I was excited to move to Washington and attend law school. Then one day, my sponsor came and asked me why I had not applied to attend any of the Ivy League law schools. I told him for two reasons: one I didn't have Ivy League law school money, and two, even if I did, I probably couldn't get accepted.

My sponsor had to remind me of what my dad had always told me. "You will never know if you never try." My sponsor explained to me that most of these schools had set aside fellowship money for students just like me. My roommate and I were both inspired and applied. With the help of my sponsor and his glowing recommendations, my roommate and I were both accepted at the prestigious Cornell University School of Law.

About two weeks before we were scheduled to pack our bags and move to Ithaca, New York, the campus of Cornell University, my roommate changed his mind. He had decided to put law school on hold. I felt like all my plans had just gone up in smoke because I was not going that far by myself.

The following day I immediately contacted Howard University to renew my interest in attending their school. I was informed that since I had not followed through on my acceptance letter, my position had been awarded to another student.

I was devastated with no directions; I turned to my dad, who somehow always had some wisdom and an answer. My dad had met James Bullock in Jackson, Mississippi, during one of his pastor's conferences. James Bullock was from Jackson, Mississippi, and was the Dean of admissions at Texas Southern University Law School in Houston, Texas. My dad said he would give Dean Bullock a call.

Dean Bullock told my dad their university had already accepted all the students they were going to accept for the coming year but told me to submit my application anyway because there would probably be a student who had been accepted would cancel. I submitted my application on the following Monday as Dean Bullock had suggested.

Dean Bullock said there would generally be one or two students who had been accepted for various reasons wouldn't show. He assured me that I would get the first slot that was not filled. On the following Thursday, I received the call from Dean Bullock with the good news. I knew then that was where God probably wanted me to be anyway.

Four years later, I was able to walk across the stage at Marshall School of Law, a law school I had been instrumental in helping name and awarded a Juris Doctorate degree. My dad was so proud but was not able to attend because of another emergency but did call to congratulate me and say, "Son, I told you, you are the one." I had become, because of my dad's encouragement, the first Walter Hays heir to receive an advanced degree.

Yes, I was the one for my dad's dream, but not the only one. My dad encouraged and challenged all his eight children to try to find that special and unique purpose they were created for and to accomplish their God-created goal. Go on to college was what my dad said should be the first step in determining one's purpose, and most of his children did. There was no college money for any of us, but my dad believed and passed on down to all his children, "*Where there is a will, God will provide a way.*"

There was another unjust and dehumanizing experience that had an impact on my family. This experience would cause another Steadman Hays's son to be called upon and challenged by my dad to step outside his comfort zone and go to medical school to become a doctor.

Some of my siblings including myself were born in my father's house except for the younger ones that were born after integration. My hometown, Mendenhall, Mississippi, had one hospital, and that hospital was segregated. This meant, if you were Black and needed medical attention or care, you were not allowed in the hospital unless you went through the humiliation of going to the basement through the back door.

Most Black children were born in homes, delivered by midwives. To this day, there is still some confusion what year I was born because many midwives were not educated and kept poor records. My mother related that since my birthday was on December 27 during the Christmas holiday celebrations, the midwife that helped deliver me rushed after my delivery to be back with her family and never made any records of my birth. It really didn't matter too much anyway because at the time, Black lives were not valued by the authorities in my hometown.

As a result, many years later, my mother said I was born one year and my dad said another. I was not the only Black person born in Mississippi during this time that did not get a birth certificate. There were many others. Just as many Black babies were not accounted for, there were also many Black people that died or just disappeared without an official record, or an unsubstantiated fact record would be filed. Black lives really did not matter in many cases for some.

There were a lot of swamps and untraveled backwoods in Mississippi. My granddad and his family owned several hundred acres of land that was seldom traveled on. It has been reported that people would just go into one of those back woods and never be seen again. They would be reported as just disappeared.

Just as birth certificates for some Black people were either not prepared or prepared unprofessionally and under questionable circumstances, so were death certificates for Blacks in Mississippi. There were a lot of Blacks that died in Mississippi under what would normally be questionable circumstances but would be ruled natural causes by a person without any medical or forensic knowledge. This would also happen to my dad.

It was once reported a Black man in Mississippi stepped outside the code died after being shot twenty-three times. The local coroner, without any inquest or investigation as to the cause of death, ruled, "The boy died as a result of the worst case of suicide I have ever seen."

It has also been reported that a Black man was pulled out of the Pearl River (a known cemetery for a lot of Black men that stepped out of line in Mississippi) after the Klan had placed four cement blocks and twenty-five pounds of chain around his neck. The local coroner ruled, "The boy stole more cement blocks and chain than he could swim with."

Another example of how Black lives didn't matter in Mississippi was, I never had an official birth certificate until I entered law school. I was born during the Christmas holidays and the midwife that delivered me never filed the birth documents. My dad was able to get some local doctor to prepare one for me based on information my dad gave him twenty some years after the fact when I was not able to enter law school without one.

Medical School

My dad, Steadman Hays, did not just sit around complaining about Mississippi's racist unjust system that would not permit his wife to have her babies in an updated medical facility, again encouraged my younger brother Gregory Hays to go to medical school. Because of an unjust system, my younger brother Gregory also stepped outside his comfort zone, attended medical school, and is now one of the top medical doctors in the country today. He has also provided the medical world with his inventions to save lives and to improve medical procedures.

The Hays family is so proud of Dr. Gregory Hays and his accomplishments. His life is just another example of what God can do even under unbelievable circumstances when one is willing to step outside their comfort zone and follow the plan God has for their life.

The racist, unjust legal system would not allow my dad and many other African Americans access to the legal system, and the racist, unjust medical system would not allow my mother and many other African American women to even have their babies delivered in an adequate medical facility. The system meant it for evil, but God used it as good to encourage my dad to inspire and encourage his children and others to not just talk and protest but to do something positive about the situation.

The Military

Psychologists generally agree that a normal child's brain continues to develop until about twenty-five years of age. My dad, Steadman Hays, was not a psychologist, but he must have understood this fact. My dad insisted that all his boys either enrolled in college or the military after finishing high school because he did not believe we were ready at that age to take on the world.

My dad had come from a great military family. He and his four brothers served in the military during World War II. His oldest brother, Roosevelt Hays, was a decorated war hero. My oldest brother, Steadman Hays Jr., knew he had to follow Dad's rule of enrolling in college or joining the military and decided he had a hard enough time just getting through high school, so college was not for him; he joined the military. Dwight followed suit and was shipped off to Vietnam where he had to grow up fast defending this country. He survived and has done quite well in his career choice and now lives on a resort. Michael Hays, the younger brother, also followed suit and volunteered for the Navy. After four years, I guess he still had not completely grown up, so he joined the Army. Gregory, the youngest brother, also did his tour before finishing medical school. I guess, I am the only Steadman Hays son that could have but did not join the military.

My dad answered his call from God and did a good job inspiring his children and others to answer their call from God and carry on when he, my dad, was no longer around to lead the charge. My dad tried to prepare his children to be ready when he would be called by God for another mission and would no longer be with us.

We Always Expected That Dreadful Call (RIP, Rev. Steadman Hays)

The Steadman Hays family growing up in Mississippi in the '60s and '70s lived with and was constantly receiving dreadful, threatening, and annoying telephone calls. These calls generally informed the family of some tragedy that had happened to one of my dad's friends or fellow civil rights workers, like the call we received concerning the murder of my dad's friend and coworker Medgar Evers.

Sometimes the calls would be a threatening call for my dad from some sick racist that was opposed to what my dad was doing to promote civil rights or for what he stood for. If the call came when my dad was not home, we all prayed it was not a call to inform us about some tragedy that had happened to him. If my dad was home, we knew it was from another sick-minded racist making another threat on my dad's life.

Years passed and things seemed to be getting better all over the South. It appeared the lynchings were becoming less and hopefully a thing of the past. Black and White people were living, working, and getting along much better. The civil rights movement had made some major changes to improve a better life for all.

By this time, all of my dad's children had all grown up and moved away except for the youngest, Greg, who was still in college. My dad however continued to be involved in the community. He was always involved in the political process. Most politicians would do whatever they could to get my dad's support and endorsement. My dad even ran for a political office himself.

About this time there was a sheriff in my hometown running for reelection that my dad would not support or endorse because of his questionable dealings, his racist views, and the way he had mistreated Black citizens. My dad publicly and actively campaigned against him. Then one day, my dad received a telephone call supposedly from one of the sheriff's supporters telling my dad he would not live to see the election.

A few days after my dad received that call from the sheriff's supporter, my mother was at work when she received that dreadful call the Hays family had lived in fear of one day receiving. The caller informed my mother that my dad had been killed. My mother said she ignored the call and continued working because she believed this was just another one of the many annoying and harassing calls she had received over the years from hateful anonymous callers.

My mother said she knew this was not just another harassing call because a few minutes later, she saw my dad's oldest brother, Roosevelt Hays, approaching her job. She realized that something was terribly wrong for her brother-in-law Roosevelt to come to her job. My mother's brother-in-law broke the news to informed her that my dad had in fact really been killed this time.

Over the next few minutes, each one of my dad's children from Michigan, Illinois, Louisiana, Texas, Florida, and Mississippi received that dreadful call. I will never forget where I was and what I was doing when I received my call. I was at work on the night shift in Dallas, Texas, when my wife called and said I needed to come home because something had happened.

I drove home about fifteen miles away at record speed not knowing what to expect when I arrived home. At the time I was working two jobs. I had just begun trying to develop a law practice by day and worked about fifteen miles away from home at a General Motor's warehouse at night. I was on my night job when I received the call.

I arrived home and was relieved to see my wife and two small children were all fine, but then my wife had to tell me my dad had been killed. I immediately called my older sister Evelyn to see if she knew any details. She was so upset and emotional until I could get very little information from her. I then called my mom.

My dad had prepared my mom for this moment. She was a civil rights activist's wife in Mississippi and knew the danger. She was a pastor's wife and a great performer and actress. Over the years, my dad had pastored several churches. My mom had to be a pastor's wife and first lady as many referred to her whether she wanted to or not.

I am sure there were many times in her life over the years where she had to smile when she felt like crying. I am sure there were times she had to show strength when her heart was breaking. This was one of those times. She was a pastor's wife, and she played her role well.

My dad prepared all of his family for the day the curtains would close, the audience would be gone, and my mom would be on stage alone. I knew this would be the time my mom would need that strength my dad could no longer provide her with. I knew her children needed to be there by her side when the curtains closed and reality set in. My mom left the protection of her mother and father and had been married to my dad since she was a teenager. She had never experienced being alone before.

My mom played her role so well that if I had not known the despair, the loneliness, the brokenness her heart must have been going through, I would not have known she was dying inside. My mom was putting on a great act of strength for her family. She was the strong one that was able to keep everything together.

After I had talked to my mom, I called my other brothers and sister. They were all making preparation to travel back to Mississippi to deal with this tragedy. I started to leave that same night but then realized my mother would need someone there after her guests and other children had gone and the reality sunk in. I waited another day to take care of business at home in order for me to be able to spend a week or so with my mom after everyone had gone. I knew that would be the time she would no longer be able to wear the disguise of that strong, in-control woman.

After I had made all the necessary arrangements, I arrived in Mississippi the following day. All the other siblings were already there. I had delayed my arrival because I knew I needed to be there when my mother needed me the most; that would be when the last act was over, the curtains closed, and she could step from the stage she had performed so well on back into reality.

The first thing I did after arriving in Mississippi and making sure my mom was okay was to try to find out what happened to my dad. My mom appeared to be as calm and collected as if nothing had happened, but I knew this was her front she was putting on to protect her children. We were told my dad had been killed in a tractor accident.

My dad was not a rich man, but in his retirement years, he had purchased a very expensive tractor that he loved to show off. It was his grown-up toy. On the day of the alleged accident, my dad was supposed to have been bush hauling around a relative's lake when his tractor allegedly turned over on him. The alleged accident occurred about a mile off the main road in a secluded area about a mile and a half from our home.

The alleged accident raised a lot of questions, because the first person to the accident scene was the same sheriff that my dad was campaigning against and had received the alleged threat that my dad would not live to see the election from one of his supporters. The other issues that were raised were the way the case was handled.

My dad's oldest brother, Roosevelt Hays, lived about a mile and a half from the accident scene. He was home at the time, but no one told him about the accident. My dad's brother Roosevelt said he saw the sheriff and other law enforcement vehicles pass his house going toward the accident scene and became concerned about what had transpired.

The sheriff normally did not come to that part of town unless something was going on. My dad's brother said he became more suspicious when he saw a city ambulance and the local coroner go by about an hour later. He said he knew something serious must be happening.

My dad's brother said he decided to drive down to investigate what was going on. He said when he arrived at the entrance off the main road, he was stopped by some law enforcement officers and told he could not go down that road because it was a crime/accident scene.

According to my dad's brother Roosevelt, the sheriff and his deputies kept everyone from the crime/accident scene for over two hours before they brought my dad's body out. No one was allowed to see either my dad or the accident/crime scene for hours except the sheriff and his deputies.

My sister Evelyn, who had arrived from Illinois, said she went to the funeral home the following day to see my dad's body. She said the staff at the funeral home initially would not allow her to see him because the sheriff's office had told the funeral home staff they were still investigating and not to allow anyone to see him. She said after much demanding and her strong emotional reactions, they finally gave in and allowed her to see him. She proceeded to say that he appeared to have been so disfigured to the point she did not recognize him. Evelyn had arrived in Mississippi from Illinois the day after my dad had been killed.

As soon as I arrived from Texas the following day and had gotten settled in, I went to the funeral home to see my dad. I was told by the funeral home staff that I would not be able to see him because there were major cosmetic reconstruction procedures that had to be performed before anyone would be allowed to see him.

The following morning, I informed the funeral home staff I would get a court order if they did not allow me to see my dad. I was then told my dad's body had been transferred to Jackson, some thirty miles away, because the cosmetic procedure had to be performed by a specialist in Jackson. We were told we would be allowed to see him once the procedure was finished.

That same day, my brother Steadman Jr. took me to where the accident was supposed to have happened. The accident scene did not appear to me to have happened the way the sheriff had described it. But this was Mississippi and my dad was a Black man who had crossed the line and not followed the code many times in his life. He had survived many attempts on his life in the past. The family had to come to grips with and accept that this was within God's will.

Over the next few days, as people poured in from across the state, paid their visits, and gave their condolences, I observed my mom in her role as pastor's wife. Rather than being consoled, she put on her first lady's face and was consoling her guests. I believe this was the way she dealt with her grieving heart.

I was a little disappointed that some people were still depending on my mom to be the hostess and meet their needs. This should have been the time my mom was being served rather than my mom serving them. But my mom would not have had it any other way.

I never got a chance to see my dad until they brought his body to the church for his funeral. My oldest sister Evelyn would be the only family member that got a chance to see him before he was funeralized. They claimed it took them that long to get him ready. My sister Evelyn and I wanted to have an autopsy and investigation done, but my dad's brother Roosevelt told us to let it be.

Uncle Roosevelt used a lot of wisdom when he said, "Would you rather live your life wondering what really happened to your dad or live your life knowing what happened and knowing nothing was going to be done about it?"

My dad had a great homecoming celebration. I remember standing at the entrance door to the church with my dad's brother Uncle Roosevelt Hays, watching the church parking lot fill up with cars and then seeing as far as one could see on both sides of the road, cars lined up trying to show their final respect for my dad's funeral. Uncle Roosevelt, my dad's oldest brother, turned to me and said, "You and I won't have this many people coming to our funeral. You should be proud—your dad was a great man."

Dad, I am so proud. You were truly a great man. Dad, you fought a good fight, you finished your race, you kept the faith; henceforth there is laid up for you a crown of righteousness (2 Tim. 4). If I could only see you now; for I am sure you are prancing around heaven wearing your crown with such pride. Dad, RIP.

When Death Comes Calling
Carl Hays

When death comes calling, don't be afraid or send him away.
Death has a message from God, so death is okay.
Death has a message from God; your job here is done and the victory is won.
So, come celebrate with your Father, the Holy Ghost, and his Son.
Death is not your enemy; he's your friend.
Death is a wonderful new beginning, not the end.
Death comes to bring peace, rest, and to relieve all pain.
Death comes to bring eternal happiness in Jesus's name.
The grave has no victory and death no sting.
For Jesus said he took care of all those things.
From the cross, he said it's all finally finished.
So, you can stand before my Father totally unblemished.
When death comes calling, don't be afraid or send him away.
Death has a message from God, so death is okay.
Your Father sent you here to work a little while.
But now wants you in heaven to join his heavenly crowd.
Tell your loved ones and friends not to mourn.
For you heard the voice of Jesus saying softly and tenderly come home.
And when we look and see your star smiling in the night sky.
It will be a message for us not to fear when it's our time to die.
For he promised us he would go and prepare a place for us.
And we can join you and him someday if we only trust.
But in the meanwhile, we must to carry on.
Until we too hear the voice of Jesus saying softly and tenderly come home. And it's said the joy we'll share as we tarry there.
We'll surely find that none other can compare.
So, when death comes calling, don't be afraid or send him away.
Death has a message from God, so death is okay.

How Do We Apply These Stories?

The biblical stories, the civil rights leaders' stories, and the Hays family story should be an encouragement and inspiration to anyone facing difficulties in life that God is and has always been just and faithful. During the many hardships and difficulties the Hays family faced, I never once remember my dad giving up or teaching his family to hate those who were attempting to inflict the hardships on the family. It was my dad's teachings that helped his family be able to cope with the many attacks on his family and how to overcome some of the most difficult times in American history.

My dad used these attacks and difficulties as motivation to continue the struggle and taught his family that God may allow you to go through some hardships so that he can prepare you for his use. He always taught his family that God is faithful and always knows just how much one can bear. The encouraging thing my dad taught is found in one of my favorite Bible verses of encouragement: "No temptation has overtaken you except what is common to mankind. And God is faithful; he will not let you be tempted beyond what you can bear; but when you are tempted, he will also provide a way out so that you can endure it" (1 Cor. 10:13).

Just like many of the biblical characters went through many hardships and in some cases unthinkable suffering, God was still in control. In many cases, God was using their trials as a test or as preparations for the job God had for them. Steadman Hays most certainly had his share of testing and suffering during his life, but he always taught his family, no matter what the situation, to trust in God. I think today, each one of Steadman Hays's children, if given the chance, would say, "Thank you and well done, Dad. You fought a good fight, you kept the faith, you finished your course."

One of the main lessons I learned from my dad, Steadman Hays, and would like to pass on was when I told my dad that only one in ten thousand in my situation could accomplish what he had dreamed for me and his response was, "Son, you are looking at the wrong number. You are looking at the ten thousand. Son, you are the one." Steadman Hays would say, when you are facing the insurmountable odds in life such as a million to one, remember the same one that made the million also made the one.

God Always Has the Last Say

My dad is gone, but his teachings live on. My dad taught his family that there will be a lot of things in life we won't understand. He taught us that there would be a lot of things that we will feel are unfair, but we should do everything as if we were doing them for God and not because of or for man.

My dad taught us that God uses people who are willing to step outside their comfort zone for his purpose. I have always tried to teach my children, like my dad taught us, the principles of doing everything as if you are doing them for God, but I must admit, I have not always been faithful and trusting enough to be used by God in all circumstances.

The times I have trusted God and allowed God to use me, he has always been faithful. I try to teach and give my children some of the many examples and experiences in my personal life when I trusted God rather than leaning on my own understanding (Prov. 3:5–6) and it has always paid off. One of the main areas in my life where I have tried to apply these principles has been in the work force.

My dad always taught his family to work hard and do the best you can on any and every job you may be assigned regardless of how your employer may treat you, because you are not working for the employer; you are working for God, and God always has the last say. Your employer may mistreat you for a while, but in the end, God is the final judge of your deeds and will reward you for your faithfulness.

There is no better illustration of this principle than in the biblical life story of Joseph from the book of Genesis. Joseph had been betrayed by his brothers, sold into slavery, and worked as a slave in Egypt. He worked faithfully and accepted his condition until God helped him find favor with Potiphar.

Pharaoh eventually, because of Joseph's faithfulness, hard work, and God's hand upon him, promoted Joseph to the position of chief administrator over all of Egypt. Joseph was now second in command over the most powerful country in the world. Joseph's former bosses, slave masters, and even his brothers that had betrayed him had to now become footstools at his feet. "Sit at my right hand until I make your enemies a footstool for your feet" (Ps. 110:1).

Work As If You Are Working for God, Not for Man (Col. 3:23)

Steadman Hays, my dad, may be gone but he continues to live as long as those of us he touched and influenced continue to believe in and follow his examples and teachings. One of the main lessons I learned from my dad was to always work hard for what you desired. I was taught by my dad to always work hard and do a good job regardless of the circumstances, because in the end, God would always have the last say. If God has the last say, then why should we be concerned with what an employer does and can do?

One example that has made an everlasting impact on my life was when I was trying to work my way through law school. I had been awarded a fellowship that paid for all my tuition and for my expensive law books, but I still had basic needs; food, clothing, and shelter. My parents were struggling just to support themselves and my younger siblings, so I could not expect any financial help from them. It was very difficult finding a job that would coincide with my rigorous law school schedule.

The first job I was able to find that would coincide with my schedule was a job as a cashier at a major supermarket. The store employed a lot of college students to work as cashiers and had flexible schedules, which I needed. I was assigned to work from 4:00 p.m. to midnight.

The store would be very busy at the beginning of my shift from about 4:00 p.m. until about 9:00 p.m. Between 9:00 p.m. and closing there would be very few customers coming in the store, which meant the cashiers had a lot of downtime.

Most of the cashiers were young White female students that would often hang out at my cash register during downtime. My White supervisor didn't like to see those White girls hanging out with me at my cash register, so he came to me one night and told me when the store was not crowded to go and straighten out merchandise on the shelves.

I knew this was a stocker's job and not part of my job description, and I also knew my supervisor was discriminating because no other cashier was required to do this. I didn't complain; I just did as instructed until one night a few weeks later the general store manager just happened to drop by the store. When he saw me in the store being the only cashier straightening up the merchandise, he approached and said, "I like your employee attitude."

The following day I was called into the general manager's office and was offered a new position in the store as the night shift assistant manager. This was a great opportunity because of more money and a better schedule. This job worked well for me until the end of the semester, which meant a new class schedule. I had to resign because of conflict with school and work.

I finally found another job as a field supervisor trainee with a major janitorial company. I was so disappointed when I had to resign from the other job, but I remembered when I got the new job, something my mother once said, "When one door is closed, God will open a better door." I was so happy to find the new job and hoped what my mother had said would come true.

I was assigned to travel around the Houston, Texas, metroplex with a senior field supervisor for three months as a trainee. After the three-month training period, I would be promoted to a field supervisor. A field supervisor's job was to travel to the various job sites to make sure everything was in order and all employees assigned to him showed up for work and did their jobs.

Each field supervisor with the company was given a certain area to be responsible for and a staff of employees. Each field supervisor was given a number of job sites and budget to manage. The field supervisor would be responsible for paying for supplies and employees' salaries out of his budget.

On my first night on the job, I traveled with my field supervisor/trainer to several buildings. We arrived at one building where one of his employees had called in sick. When this happens, the field supervisor is supposed to call the main office for additional help. This additional help would be paid out of the field supervisor's budget. Rather than calling the main office for additional help, my field supervisor/trainer asked me if I would be willing to fill in for the employee that had called in sick. Since I was being paid out of another budget, my salary would not come out of my trainer's budget. I knew this was not part of a trainee's job, but I didn't complain and agreed to do it anyway.

The following night, I met my field supervisor/trainer, and we started making our rounds. We arrived at another building and discovered that one employee had not shown up for work. My field supervisor/trainer again asked me if I minded filling in for his employee that had not shown up. Again, I didn't complain but did the job that another person should have done. This happened every night for the entire week until that Friday night.

My trainer had left me in this big building to clean it up alone. I had been cleaning up this office building from about 7:00 p.m. until about 2:00 a.m. when I noticed the owner of the company coming down the hall. This was very unusual because the owner rarely came out at night and especially on a Friday night.

When the owner saw me in that building alone cleaning toilets and mopping floors, he asked, "Aren't you Carl Hays, the law student?" I said yes. He said, "You are supposed to be a field supervisor trainee, but you are willing to mop floors and clean toilets." I said yes. He then asked what I had done the previous nights. I told him the same as tonight. He then asked if I could be in his office early Monday morning.

On Monday morning, I met with the owner of the company. He informed me that my three-month training period had been canceled and beginning today I would begin as a regular field supervisor replacing the field supervisor that was supposed to have been training me.

This was an answered prayer and another example of how being humble and working as for the Lord and not for man had paid off, not only was it almost twice the money I was making as a trainee, it also gave me the opportunity for the much-needed time to study. Now I could set my own schedule and have more time to study. God really does always have the last say. And, Mom, I guess you were right again.

As a field supervisor, I was given a crew, a budget, and an area of the city to be responsible for. It allowed me time to study in between checking on my crew. This was the perfect job for my situation, for my schedule. Being humble and working as if I were working for God and not for man (Col. 3:23) had paid off again.

Another example of being patient and allowing God to work out a situation would happen a few years later when I joined the Dallas County Public Defender's Office as a staff attorney. I was the first and only African American attorney employed in the Dallas County Public Defender's Office. The office had a policy of naming the top-performing attorney as the attorney of the year. I had the best record in performance in the office my first year. The Attorney of the Year Award however went to another attorney.

I felt shunned but I never complained. I continued to do my job the way my dad had always taught me, "to work as if I were working for the Lord not for man" (Col. 3:23–24). The following year, I was awarded the Attorney of the Year Award, but not just that, a few years later, I was appointed as the first African American Director of a Public Defender's office in the State of Texas. I was now, through the grace of God and his faithfulness, in charge of the entire office.

I always tell my children when they come to me complaining about their jobs or how they are being mistreated some of my many experiences in life and how God has always been faithful. I always try to explain to them, the job they are complaining about is a job many others are praying they had. I try to explain to them about some of the many difficult jobs their grandfather had to perform, being mistreated and discriminated against without having any legal recourse. I try to explain to them that this was the way their great-grandfather had earned some of those nonacademic degrees by accepting his situation but working hard to change the situation in order to make things better for himself and others.

I try to teach them that we sometimes find ourselves complaining about things we have no control over, and sometimes God has something better in mind for us if we just be content and faithful. I remind them about my running for district judge. I had the best qualifications, the most endorsements, and more experience than all the other candidates put together and should have won but lost.

The judgeship I lost would have been for a four-year term. During the campaign, I had met some very prestigious and influential people including Texas Governor George W. Bush, who would later become president of the United States. My wife and I were invited to the governor's inauguration as well as the presidential inauguration. I would later, because of this experience, be invited to serve in Governor Bush's administration and was invited to apply for a presidential appointment post.

I also met some people who would be instrumental in getting me appointed as a judge for the city of Dallas where I served until I resigned in good standing fifteen years later. The judgeship I thought I wanted would have only been for four years. I didn't know at that time, but a big political change was about to take place in Dallas, Texas. The political party I was running in was about to lose power, and all who won that year would become unemployed and would lose their office the next election.

I was so disappointed losing at the time but could not see the ram God had in the bush waiting for me. God had something far better for me than what I could see. Sometimes we must just trust and wait upon the Lord. "Those that wait upon the Lord shall renew their strength; they shall mount up with wings as eagles" (Isa. 40:31).

In defeat, I was victorious. In my defeat, I had established many important contacts that would open up many opportunities for me. One of the contacts I made offered me an adjunct professor position with the Peace Maker's Ministry where I would have traveled with the ministry all around the world teaching peace-making principles. It was a great opportunity for me, but I did not want to be away from my family for such long periods of time, so I declined the offer.

I did however agree and accepted a short-term teaching assignment trip to Africa where we met with church and civic leaders from sixteen different African countries and taught them the peace-making principles. We taught in Johannesburg, the University of Zambia, and many other Southern African cities.

My dad had always taught his children to be the best you can be and trust God to do the rest. He taught us "to demand what you are worth but be worth what you demand." I have tried to live by those principles, and I can see now how they have really paid off in my life.

My dad didn't live long enough to witness many of the things he dreamed, predicted, and tried to accomplish in his own life, but I can truly say that I am a product of his visions, inspirations, and teachings and would not have been able to accomplish many of my life goals if it had not been for those many dinner table prayer meetings and lectures.

My dad also taught his family more than just life accomplishments; he also taught us to do our best and then to be content with what position God has placed us in and to do our best in that position but to never be afraid to step outside our comfort zone when necessary.

My dad taught us that God will sometimes allow us to go through things to test us, to prepare us, and sometimes to discipline us for our mistakes. Many people live an unhappy, uncontented life because they fail to accept and be content with the position God has placed them in. These were some of the principles my dad tried to teach his family.

I was, as an example, perfectly happy with the new suit I had on until I saw someone with a nicer one. Rather than being thankful for my suit, I was envying the one my neighbor had. I was perfectly happy with my car until I saw someone with a newer one. Rather than being thankful for the blessing of having a car, I was envying the one my neighbor had. I was perfectly happy with my home until I saw someone with a bigger one. My sirloin steak was delicious until I looked across the table and saw someone with a porterhouse steak. My dad taught us that we should always give thanks for what we have been blessed with and not envy what others have.

The apostle Paul in his letter to the church at Philippi talked about living a content life. Paul lived in constant danger from both his own countrymen and his opposition. Many did not like the message he was delivering. Paul spent a considerable amount of time in prison, he was beaten many times, he was shipwrecked and abandoned, he was bitten by a serpent, he also had a thorn in his flesh, but through it all Paul said, "I have learned the secret of being content in any and every situation" (Phil. 4:12).

We will never be happy with our station in life until we learn how to be content with what we have and where God has placed us in life. The Bible tells us, "Therefore I tell you, do not worry about your life, what you will eat or drink, or about what you will wear or about your body" (Matt. 6:25).

Sometimes God uses the most unexpected people and allows us to be placed in certain situations to prepare the way for others just as John the Baptist, the most unexpected, who wore camel hair and ate locusts and wild honey, prepared the way for Jesus (Mark 1:6). God often uses our family and sometimes just ordinary people to prepare the way for us and others.

My dad did not personally accomplish a lot of the goals he set for his children, but he most certainly prepared the way for his children and others to accomplish goals by building bridges so we could dream dreams we would never have imagined accomplishing had it not been for his vision, teachings, inspiration, and the preparing of the way by my father,

Steadman Hays. My dad was truly a bridge builder in every sense of the word.

One of my favorite and inspiring poems, "The Bridge Builder" by Will Allen Dromgoole, could have been written about my dad.

The Bridge Builder
by
Will Allen Dromgoole

An old man going a lone highway
Came, at the evening cold and gray,
To a chasm vast and deep and wide.
Through which was flowing a sullen tide.
The old man crossed in the twilight dim,
The sullen stream had no fear for him;
But he turned when safe on the other side.
And build a bridge to span the tide.
"Old man," said a fellow Pilgrim near,
"You are wasting your strength with building here;
Your journey will end with ending day,
You never again will pass this way;
You've crossed the chasm, deep and wide,
Why build this bridge at evening tide?"
The builder lifted his old gray head;
"Good friend, in the path I have come," he said,
"There followed after me to-day
A youth whose feet must pass this way.
This chasm that has been as naught to me
To that fair-haired youth may a pitfall be;
He, too, must cross in the twilight dim;
Good friend, I am building this bridge for him!"

My dad, Steadman Hays, most certainly built many, many bridges for his family and others to cross. It was my dad's vision, prayers, and inspiration that built a bridge that inspired me to enter law school, my younger brother Greg to enter medical school, my other sisters and brothers to follow and fulfill their dreams, and the many others he inspired that have crossed their bridges and accomplished the things we did when it appeared to be impossible at the time.

It was only through my dad's prayers, vision, encouragement, and teachings to always be the best that you can be that I was able to become an attorney. It was also through my dad's prayers, vision, inspiration, and teachings and God's grace that I would later be invited to be the commencement speaker for a local college graduating class where I would be able to encourage those graduates by telling the class about my bridge-builder father.

When the Dean of the college got up to introduce me, he began to highlight and boost my credentials. He said, "Ladies and Gentlemen, Graduating Class, we are honored tonight to have as our commencement speaker, Mr. Carl Hays. Mr. Hays has earned and been awarded a bachelor of science degree and a jurist doctorate degree. Mr. Hays was awarded the Public Defender of the Year Award his second year on the job. He later became the first African American to be appointed over a public defender's office in the state of Texas. That office is now the largest in the state."

The Dean went on to say, "Mr. Hays has also been a certified lecturer for the State Bar of Texas, an instructor for both the Dallas Police Department and the Dallas County Sheriff's Office. Mr. Hays as the public defender was often requested to serve on many boards and to be guest speaker at many occasions including schools, community organizations, and was even invited to go to Africa where he, along with the Peace Makers Ministry, taught the peace-making principles to church and civic leaders from sixteen different African countries."

The Dean continued his introduction by stating, "As the public defender of the largest Public Defender's Office in the state of Texas, Mr. Hays was guest TV legal analyst for the most watched and famous murder trial in the country's history, the O. J. Simpson murder trial. Mr. Hays has also been the recipient of numerous other recognitions and awards including being awarded the Alumni of the Year from his high school, his undergraduate school, and his law school. Mr. Hays has also been inducted into the University of Texas at Arlington African American Hall of Fame, the Alpha Beta Kappa Honor Society, and has been inducted and is listed as one of the top attorneys in North America."

After sitting there and witnessing such an extremely impressive, awesome, and glowing introduction, I had to step off cloud nine, attempt to deflate my out-of-control flowing ego, dismiss from my mind that I had made my mark in history, and attempted to walk to the podium. I had to explain that God creates all his children with certain talents, and if it had not been for my dad's prayers, vision, inspiration, and encouragement, I would never have dreamed of accomplishing half of the things the Dean just stated in his introduction.

I have always been thankful for what my dad did to inspire his family and others to accomplish, but I will always remember the most important lesson my dad taught. My dad always taught his family that it's okay to accept and be proud of accomplishments but never so proud that we forget that only through God's grace were these accomplishments made possible.

I always realize, my accomplishments were not just because of me, because if it had not been for those bridges my dad and others built, I, as well as so many others, would not have been able to accomplish the many things we did. Many of us had very little chances or hope of accomplishing very much in life, having grown up in a small, obscure town in Mississippi.

My dad taught his family that God put us all at a special time and a special place in history to perform a special purpose. My dad always said, if God calls you for a special purpose, he will also provide a special person or something to show you and provide the way. That person for me was my dad.

My dad was a great man that built many bridges and did a lot for his family and his community but never got a lot of the recognition and invitations like some of those he paved the way for would receive. He never got an invitation to attend a governor's or a presidential inauguration, but my wife, Rhonda, and I were one of the few African Americans to have been invited to a gubernatorial inauguration and a presidential inauguration all because of the bridges my dad built.

In addition, Steadman Hays probably never got an invitation to speak at a major college or university, but because of his prayers, vision, and inspiration, his son has been and was even invited to be the keynote speaker at a local college commencement program. Because of bridges built by Steadman Hays, I also had the privilege and honor of appearing on the same platform and having been asked to introduce Ambassador Alan Keyes, a United States presidential candidate. My dad, Steadman Hays, built many bridges for many to cross, but he always taught us that man may build bridges, but never forget, God provides the way to cross.

My dad spent many years during his lifetime working with Dr. Martin L. King Jr. trying to build bridges and help create a better world for his family and community. There were many civil rights campaigns they had been involved in together during those turbulent, dangerous years of civil rights. I'm sure my dad would be very proud that I recently had the privilege and pleasure to have met and discussed issues with one of the sons of Dr. Martin L. King Jr.

Rev. Peter Johnson, also worked very closely with Dr. King during the civil rights era, introduced me as a young college student back in 1968 to Dr. Martin L. King Jr. Rev. Johnson had invited Dr. King to come to Dallas, Texas, to lead a civil rights march but discovered Dallas was not ready for Dr. King or civil rights. Dallas, unlike most Southern cities, was a very much closed city when it came to civil rights.

At the time, Dallas politics and leadership were pretty much controlled by the "White Citizens Council." Most elected officials and office holders would not dare go against the citizen council for fear of not getting reelected or not being reappointed. The council would also select a few Black ministers, similar to what the slave master did during slavery, and give them a few crumbs to keep the other Blacks in line.

Therefore, when Dr. King came to Dallas, few, if any, so-called leaders or Black ministers showed up or supported Dr. King the way he was supported in most other cities. Most of Dr. King's participants ended up being young students like me. Most of Dallas's Black ministers and so-called leaders did not support Dr. King's trip to Dallas and labeled him as an outside agitator in payback for their thirty pieces of silver.

After all these years, Rev. Johnson and I just happen to end up officing in the same Bank of America building. Not long ago, Rev. Johnson invited Martin L. King III to our office building. We were introduced some fifty years later after meeting his dad, Dr. Martin L. King Jr.

I know all this could not have happened based on my merits but could have only been accomplished through the works, wisdom, and influence of my father, Steadman Hays, who prepared the way by building bridges and being placed in the right place at the right time in history by the miracles and faithfulness of God. Thank you, Dad, for having the wisdom and faith you possessed to be able to communicate with God, for having the courage to step outside your comfort zone, for building the many bridges, and for preparing me to cross.

Martin L. King III and Carl Hays

Two sons of the civil rights era, Martin L. King III and Carl Hays had an opportunity to meet, discuss their dads, and other issues. In 1968 Rev. Peter Johnson invited Dr. Martin L. King Jr. to Dallas and introduced Carl Hays to Dr. King. In 2018 Rev. Peter Johnson invited Martin L. King III to Dallas and introduced Carl Hays to him.

This book is not intended to be a documentary on a boastful way a son can brag about his dad and his accomplishments in life, but it is intended to be a documentary on a bridge-builder father who built bridges so his family and many others through the grace of God could show and demonstrate what one can accomplish with the right people as examples, the right people's encouragement, the determination to succeed, the willingness to disregard the critics, and the courage to step outside one's comfort zone to answer God's call.

It is not intended to be about my dad and his accomplishments but about what my dad taught about accomplishments. "Accomplishments are not about who we are or what we have done; accomplishments are about God, who he is and what he has done" (Rev. Steadman Hays). Accomplishments are about God and what God can accomplish by using ordinary people to accomplish extraordinary things.

This book is intended to be about how we should respond when God calls upon us to step outside our comfort zone to accomplish the unique and special purpose for which God created us. It is intended to be about a bridge builder, a father that answered the call of God, stepped outside his comfort zone, and encouraged his family and others "to dream the impossible dream, to fight the unbeatable foe, to go where the brave dare not go, to reach that unreachable star."

Carl and Rhonda Hays with President George W. Bush

This book is intended to be about the grace of God and how God created each person with a unique talent and how God can use ordinary people to accomplish his will when one is willing to trust and have the courage to step outside their comfort zone and follow the call of God. It is intended to be about the many people that stepped outside their comfort zone to help in the struggle for equality for all of God's people.

In the end, it is intended to be about what the songwriter Andre Crouch's lyrics, "To God Be the Glory." And I also say, "To God be the glory, and if I have gained anything, let it go to Calvary. For only to God be the glory."

Amen!

The Committee for
The Presidential Inaugural
requests the honor of your presence
to attend and participate in the Inauguration of
George Walker Bush
as President of the United States of America
and
Richard Bruce Cheney
as Vice President of the United States of America
on Saturday, the twentieth of January
two thousand and one
in the City of Washington

Carl and Rhonda's invitation to the Presidential Inauguration

CHAPTER 13

God Calls All His Followers to Be Imitators of God

"I Have an Example for You"

In order to be imitators of God, one must be able to recognize God's voice, communicate with God, be willing to step outside his comfort zone, and understand what being an imitator of God really means (John 10:27). Jesus left heaven and put on the nature of humanity. He was born like any other child except a virgin birth. He grew up as any other child except without the sin nature. He experienced pain, hunger, thirst, loneliness, and all the other emotions that any other man experiences. He became our perfect example to imitate.

Jesus was born like any other man. He lived and worked like any other man. He faced the same problems as any other man. He was tempted like any other man but did not sin. What made Jesus different was he did not look to or follow the popular opinions of his day. Jesus did not concern himself with trying to be politically correct but rather gave us an example by living what was the truth.

Today, we find ourselves living in a society where people believe political correctness is the standard rather than what is truth and morally right or more importantly what God has set as the standard. Truth and God's standard should never have to apologize for political correctness. To be politically correct is the comfort zone for most. To stand for truth and God's standard, in many cases, when it goes against political correctness and popular opinion, requires the willingness and courage to step outside the comfort zone.

A speaker once said it best that America has gone so far liberal that what we once considered a sin and an abomination, political correctness and the liberal agenda caused America to tolerate, then accept, and now celebrate. God's truths never change. America should not tolerate or accept and most certainly not celebrate what God has called an abomination and sin.

God's standard generally requires one to step outside the norm and speak out against popular opinion. It normally requires one to step outside in faith. Just as Peter ventured outside his comfort zone when he stepped outside the boat onto water that normally would have caused him to sink, Peter's faith defied the norm and the law of buoyancy. It was Peter's faith that kept him afloat and kept him from sinking (Matt. 14:22–33). Throughout history, God has called on his people to be willing to step outside their comfort zone to perform his will.

Jesus's Sermon on the Mount, "The Beatitudes," calls for his followers to step outside their comfort zone. Praying for your enemies, turning the other cheek, blessing those that curse and persecute you, etc., are not something most feel very comfortable doing. God does not always call on us to do the things that are comfortable. God calls on us to be faithful and obedient.

Our forefathers stepped outside their comfort zone, crossed the ocean, came to this country, America, seeking a place where they could establish a government centered on godly principles and the religious freedom. The church was intended to be the integral focal point of our lives, our homes, our schools, and most certainly our government.

We have today allowed society and political correctness, the liberal agenda to replace and change the role of the church. The founding fathers gave the church the role of setting the moral agenda and standard for our society. Today that role is constantly being eroded and replaced by political correctness and the liberal special interest groups of our government.

Many of our churches have become nothing more than another social club. Many of our pastors today generally function without any authority of the Bible. Many righteous pastors today are afraid to step outside their comfort zone as did Jesus and the apostle Paul and speak up to confront and correct them. Jesus was constantly confronting the religious leaders of his day. The apostle Paul also, like Jesus, confronted Peter to his face when he saw Peter being a hypocrite (Gal. 2:11–21).

Today in many churches, God's house of prayer has become in many cases the pastor's den of thieves where prayer is a ritual ceremony to impress people rather than a glorification and supplication to God. God commanded in Matthew 6:6 to pray by going into our private closet, and after shutting the door, pray to God in private and not like the heathen by using a lot of repetitious words to impress.

I have witnessed so many people doing just the opposite of what Jesus instructed us in Matthew 6:6 to do when we pray that it is sometimes embarrassing. I see people on Sunday morning blocking the aisles so they can be seen in the church supposedly praying. As an attorney, I have been asked to pray for my clients and sometimes my client's family.

I am always more than willing and happy to pray for them and with them but will call them into a private room and pray. I see so many, including pastors, create a scene by waiting until a crowd is around, then they stand in front of the courtroom door, sometimes even blocking the entrance so that everyone can see and hear them pray. I often wonder, are they praying to God, or are they trying to be seen by the public?

Jesus said, "When you pray, you shall not be like the hypocrites. For they love to pray standing in the synagogues and on the corners of the streets, that they may be seen by men. But you, when you pray, go into your room, and when you have shut your door, pray to your Father who is in the secret place, will reward you openly."

I pray every day before I begin my day, but my praying is not in the public place. I go to my office early in the morning when no one is around and pray for my family and for the day we must face with just me and the Lord. I pray in my office with the door closed with no one around, in private just as Jesus commanded in Matthew 6:6.

Many of my prayers are done in the silent moments when I am driving my car or walking around without uttering one audible word. I speak from the privacy of my heart to God. I understand man needs audible words to be heard, but God hears the heart.

Does Matthew 6:6 mean we should never pray publicly? I think not. Matthew 6:6 only condemns the way some pray publicly. If we are just following tradition or praying to be seen or heard by others, then we shouldn't pray publicly, but Jesus prayed publicly, and so did the apostles. It is not the public praying that Matthew 6:6 condemns but the way and the reason people prayed publicly.

There are many examples of public prayer in the scripture. Solomon publicly prayed for the nation (1 Kings 8:22–23) as well as many other biblical characters. Public praying is not the issue. The issue is motive and reason. Public praying to draw attention or to impress should always be discouraged. If and when one is praying to the Lord, why does he need an audience? The scripture however states there is a time for everything (Eccl. 3:1–8). So, there are many times when public praying is appropriate.

CHAPTER 14

God Calls His Church

God Has a Light for You

"It's the church that should make a difference in America today" said Dr. Tony Evans, senior pastor of Oak Cliff Bible Fellowship Church in Dallas, Texas. Apparently, many churches in America today as well as in the past, it is and has been business as usual. It has been reported that the most segregated hour in America is 11:00 a.m. Sunday morning. So, it does not appear the church is making the difference but may be following the crowd or, even in too many cases, leading the crowd.

There are probably more churches in the poorest communities in this country than any other place. There is a church on almost every other street. But these communities suffer the highest crime rate, the highest poverty rate, and the most broken homes and are generally the worst place to raise a family. The church should be making a difference, not just inside the church's walls but also in the community.

God's Word says, even though we are in this world, God's church should not be of this world (John 15:19). We should not act as people of this world but instead should be imitators of Christ. The church should be the light on the hill that can't be hid (Matt. 5:14). Too often the church is hidden during times when the church should shine its brightest. The church, in addition to a Sunday morning sermon and a midweek prayer meeting, should address the problems in the community.

This happens mainly because most people are afraid to step outside their comfort zone and speak up. Most people will feel more comfortable following religious rituals and traditions they really don't understand or believe than doing what they truly believe if they feel their position would go against the majority or popular opinions. These people will also generally not have the knowledge to know any better or the courage to speak up themselves but will stand on the sideline and criticize those that will speak up.

This is one of the main reasons one can only ask the question, where was the light, the church, during some of the darkest moments in world history? Where was the light, the church, during one of the darkest moments in American history—slavery, the civil rights era? Where is the light, the church, today during most major crisis?

Most people in the church even today, because of their lack of knowledge and their fear, remain silent during the times the light of the church should shine its brightest. The church should consist of more than four walls. Jesus said to Peter, "Upon this rock, I'll build my church" (Matt. 16:18). Jesus was not referring to four walls.

My wife and I recently visited the Holocaust Museum in Jerusalem, Israel. There is one exhibit that has a replica of the sky with millions of stars. Each star in the replica sky represents one of the over two million babies and children that were executed by Hitler and the Nazis during the Holocaust. As I viewed this amazing and emotional exhibit and listen to the name of each child being called, I wondered, how could the world have stood by and allowed this to happen? And where was God's church, the light on the hill that could not be hidden?

But then I had to realize that even here in America, "where God has shared his grace on thee," we stand by and allow close to a million babies to be murdered each year. And that light, the church, says very little and does even less about it. Why isn't that light of the church shining in those dark abortion rooms?

I recently received a letter from Jay Sekulow, the American Center for Law and Justice (ACLJ) chief counsel, enlightened me that taxpayers of America are paying to Planned Parenthood more than $500 million per year to abort (murder) over nine hundred children a day in America. Can you believe this is happening in America?

Where was the light, the church, when I read about the 913,000 abortions that we knew about and were recorded that were performed with the government's blessing in the United States in 2015? There were probably thousands of other illegal ones we didn't know about that were not recorded. We are supposed to agree because it's a woman's body and she can do what she wants with it.

This is a false argument, because it is not her body she is murdering! It's a baby, an individual created by God. The church needs to take a stand and let its light illuminate with the truth about abortion. Today, there is a movement to allow a mother to decide before delivery of God's precious gift to abort for almost any reason. Our America is saying it's all legal and the church, the light that shouldn't be hidden, remains in the dark.

I once heard a front-runner democratic presidential candidate respond to a question that was asked by a young man. The man stated, "I was born on May 8, if my mother had wanted to abort me on May 7, would you have supported her decision to do so?" Surprisingly, the candidate got a standing ovation from the crowd when he answered he would have. How wicked has America become when we give a standing ovation for agreeing to murder a baby? Isn't this the exact same thing God destroyed Sodom and Gomorra for?

In 1992, I wrote a poem to America about abortions.

America! America!
by
Carl Hays

America! America! Please hear my cry,
before another baby must suffer and die.
Your hands are dripping like a shameful flood,
from the wombs of mother's with innocent blood.
Your sins and guilt can no longer be hid,
America! We all must now pay for what you did.
America! America! Please hear my cry,
Before another baby must suffer and die.
We dress on Sundays in our Sunday's best,
We sing and pray and even confess,
But while preachers are praying that members are paying
You call it church; but God knows you are playing.
Your sermons are great; you're teaching divine,
But we act like the Pharisees of Jesus's time.
We return home for a week of peace,
But there can be no peace until the killings cease.
America has been blessed with God's abundant grace,
America has been blessed as much as any other place.
But will the silent screams from the mother's womb,
Be the final inscription on America's tomb?
America! America please hear my cry,
Before another baby must suffer and die.
If every church in America reacted and stood,
And say it's wrong and you know you should.
For a doctor to use his medical knowledge and skills,
his training and healing powers to kill.
We know politicians are afraid to speak,
For they may lose the office they seek.
Some pastors will speak but fail to act,
And James tells us, faith without works is a losing fact.
So, if the church will humble itself and pray,
And turn from its wicked ways and say,
And call it what it is, murder, and kill no more.
So God may not judge America as Sodom and Gomorra.

The church is the last place a person should fear speaking the truth. But today, it appears the church has also taken the position of the worldly view, accepting what is politically correct even if it is biblically wrong. Many churches today appear to take the same position as do most in our society, and that is to stay within their comfort zone. To stand up and address these issues as Jesus did and as the apostle Paul and many others did would require the church leadership to step outside their comfort zone.

Many of the churches today are content and comfortable to sing a few religious songs, pray a few prayers, and listen to a Sunday morning sermon. It is what many churches today call church. There is little if any effort done to reach into the community to do what a church should be doing. That is trying to reach the lost. In far too many churches there is generally more emphasis placed on giving than on reaching.

There are many issues the church should be taking a stand on, but in most cases, the church has remained silent today. Most churches remained silent during the darkest moments in American history. Slavery, the civil rights era, abortion, and many other issues the church should have been at the forefront on, but most churches remained in the dark background and silent. The light on the hill, the church, was hidden and remains hidden today on many issues it should speak out on and expose.

There are far too many corrupt ministers (false prophets) heading churches today that Jesus and the Bible warned us about being exposed routinely in our society, but most church leaders remain silent. They probably fear attacking some of these corrupt ministers because some of these false leaders are so powerful and popular. These false leaders are therefore allowed to continue to mislead, deceive, take advantage, and prey on their misguided followers.

Some of these corrupt, powerful ministers have committed some of the most heinous, abominable, and reprehensible crimes even against small innocent children. Some have gone to prison for such heinous crimes, and when their prison term is up, they return to the pulpit, and in far too many cases, people continue to follow and to be misled by them.

The church leaders that remain silent are allowing these false leaders to mislead their followers. Jesus was constantly exposing and criticizing the corrupt and false religious leaders of his time. When the apostle Paul saw Peter, one of the most popular and powerful ministers of his day, being a hypocrite, Paul confronted him to his face and corrected him (Gal. 2:11–13). Why aren't pastors doing this today? Is it because they are afraid to step outside their comfort zone? Are they afraid they may be exposed doing the same or similar things?

The church today, because of the lack of true leadership, is losing its position as a moral standard for our society because church leaders are uncomfortable speaking the truth if it goes against the political correctness standard. Today far too many church leaders are afraid to speak out against issues they should. It appears it is more important to be politically correct than to be biblically correct.

Very few felt uncomfortable just a few years ago mentioning God in public places or beginning the day at school with a morning prayer, but today there is a movement to remove God as far away from our public lives as possible. They are trying to move God away from our schools, our government, and in some cases even our churches. Some church leaders are afraid to speak against political issues that are clearly against God's standards because of political correctness.

Parents once sent their children to school hoping their loved ones would return home without getting into a fistfight or maybe receive a referral for talking too much in class. Today parents send their children to school and can only pray they return safely rather than ending up being shot by some demented angry person that takes out his frustrations on innocent students and teachers.

Schools used to begin the day with a morning prayer and would say grace before they had their lunch. Today we have allowed political correctness and special interest groups to say this is wrong because prayer and saying grace before lunch have no place in our public schools. We have replaced the morning prayer with morning disaster drills to prepare students for what to do should some lunatic decides to come to school with a gun whose aim is to kill as many as he can. Grace before lunch has been replaced with teaching the right to alternative lifestyles.

Parents once sent their children to the one place they thought their children would be safe—the church. Today we are learning there is probably more child abuse and child molestation in the church by sex predators and child molesters than on most darkened streets. What should be the safest place today may be the worst place. These molesters find their way to places where children are and prey on these innocent children. I am sure God has a special place in hell for them.

Many churches today are worse than the ungodly churches Jesus exposed during his ministry. Many churches are no more than a den of thieves as Jesus described in his day. Many churches are so entangled with their hand in government money until they are required to adopt and follow government rules rather than following God's rules. Take government money; you must play by government rules.

Some pastors today run their church like a business, using God's house for their own personal gratification, getting rich, and doing whatever it takes to keep the money coming in. Some pastors teach about tithes and offering but fail to teach what the tithes and offerings are supposed to be used for. The tithes and offerings are supposed to be used to further God's kingdom and to take care of the widows and the poor, not to make the pastor and his family rich and famous (Deut. 26:12–13). What percentage of your church's tithes and offerings are being used to take care of the widows and poor?

Many pastors today run their church just like a chief executive officer (CEO) of a business. They are in total control of God's house. They make all the rules. They spend and decide how all the money is spent. In many cases set their own salary. The congregation is kept in the dark and has no idea what is going on. The most shameful thing is that if anyone question suspicious and wasteful spending of the budget, he/she is made to feel unspiritual for questioning their pastors or church leaders.

Pastors who are truly devoted to the ministry and spend their time as a shepherd caring for the flock entrusted to them should be compensated and have their needs met. This observation is not about them but is about the ones that enter the ministry for personal gains. This is about the pastors that have become so famous and rich off the ministry that they don't have time to shepherd the flock. They are too busy flying around the world in their private jets like a nightclub superstar.

Some pastors are not satisfied with just one private jet. Some have a fleet of private jets, custom-made cars, summer resorts, and huge compounds. One even had his doghouse air-conditioned. These pastors are prostituting the Gospel, and I am sure hell will also have a special place for them too.

Jesus told his followers to take up their cross and follow him. He did not say fill up your pockets and get as rich as you can and then follow me. Jesus's followers gave up everything they had to follow him. Jesus, the most famous minister that ever lived, would probably be ashamed to be identified with some of the ministers today that are only using the ministry to get rich and famous.

Jesus said, "The foxes have holes, the birds of the air have nests, but the Son of Man has no place to lay his head" (Luke 9:58). I wonder how many ministers today would be in the ministry if being in the ministry meant they would have no place to lay their heads.

Jesus chased the money changers out of his father's house because they were using the church to enrich themselves. What would Jesus do at your church today? In some churches there is very little difference in what Jesus saw at the church that he chased the money changers out of. Jesus said, "My father's house shall be called a house of prayer." Some churches may say, "Okay, Jesus, we will call your father's house a house of prayer, but as soon as the prayer is over, we are going to use it to make some money."

Greed and misuse of God's money is probably one of the biggest problems with the church today. Far too many false prophets are going into the ministry to get rich and famous. We hear and see almost daily some of these megachurch pastors constantly begging for funds they claim will be used for the poor, while living in multimillion-dollar estates, driving two- and three-hundred-thousand-dollar custom-made vehicles, flying private jets all in the name of the church.

I wonder how some of these pastors sleep at night knowing they just persuaded a poverty-stricken single mother on welfare to give her rent money to the church. Then, the pastor and his family misuse her offering to live in mansions like kings and queens while that mother and her family don't know where their next meal is coming from. This is in no way suggesting that poor people should not give to the church, because Jesus praised the widow for giving her last two mites (Luke 21:1). It is however an indictment against how some pastors are using the money that is being given. The Bible gives many warnings against greed and the desire to accumulate wealth (1 John 2:16). Lust comes not from the father but from the world.

> Whoever loves money never has enough; whoever loves wealth is never satisfied with their income. This too is meaningless. (Eccles. 5:10)

> Then he said to them, "Watch out! Be on your guard against all kinds of greed, life does not consist of an abundance of possessions." (Luke 12:15)

Jesus praised the woman in Mark 12:41–44 because she gave her last two mites, and Jesus made a distinction on what a person gives and why "they gave out of their wealth, but she gave out of her poverty." They gave to be seen and recognized; she gave from her heart. Hebrews 13:5 says, "Keep your minds free from the love of money." The love of money, wealth, and fame was what Satan used to tempt Jesus, and these are the number one tools Satan uses today to take down church leaders (Luke 4:1–13) (Matt. 4:1–11).

CHAPTER 15

God Calls Us to Conduct Ourselves Orderly in God's House

"I Have Instructions for You"

My father's house shall be called a house of prayer, but you are making it a den of thieves.

Matthew 21:13

In order to keep the money coming in, some pastors have allowed the worldly things to enter the church. Some will allow the worldly music and dances to attract the crowds. There was once a time when inappropriate dress was not allowed or accepted in the church, but not in some churches today.

Some say dress is not important in God's house, so let whosoever will come. Is this what God's Word says, or is this what the false prophet would lead us to believe? If the church is God's house, should there be a certain amount of respect expected? The apostle Paul most certainly gave instructions on how one should dress and conduct oneself in God's house (1 Tim. 2:9, 11–15).

Saturday night dress, Saturday nightclub music, dances, and Sunday morning music and praise service in some churches are so similar that it's hard to distinguish them. Saturday night entertainers try to appeal to the emotions rather than the intellect by playing loud music. The louder the music and the emotional appeal, the better.

There should be a difference in the appearance of God's house and the house of Satan. There should be a difference in the way we dress and conduct ourselves in God's and Satan's houses. The Bible predicted that in the last days this is exactly what would happen. People would be doing the same thing in God's house as they are doing in the house of Satan. The real problem is the Bible predicts that most will be deceived and will not even know the difference. Most will really believe they are being righteous and spiritual.

Occasionally, some people will respond to a song in church even though they have no idea what the words are as long as the rhythm of the loud music appeals to the emotions. The words of the song could actually be antichrist. There is a lot of show, screaming, loud modulating music, the louder the better, hip shaking, and we leave the nightclub and do the same thing in church.

Satan has always wanted to compete with God. Satan has done everything possible to be an imitator of God. Satan has many followers that don't even know they are following him because he is the Great Deceiver. The music and the way one responds emotionally to Satan's music and God's music should not be the same. If one cannot tell the difference, then the question should be, is this of Satan or is this of God? "Many will say to me on that day, Lord and I will say depart from me for I knew you not" (Matt. 7:22).

Back in the day when I visited the nightclubs, I would see people butt shaking and waving their hands to the loud nightclub music, and then I would see the same people in church Sunday morning butt shaking and waving their hands the same as they did in the nightclub Saturday night.

I can remember the same sexual and seductive body movements and responses to the nightclub music are so similar to the so-called worship music in some churches today. And we have the audacity to call it worshipping God. I wonder what God would call it. But far too many members are afraid to step outside their comfort zone to speak up and condemn this type of practice, so it's accepted.

Years ago, I took my daughter Sabrina, who was a child at the time, to visit a small rural church. When the preacher began to preach, he would after each sentence make a barking or hooping sound. He jumped up and danced around the pulpit like a person possessed. My daughter was so disturbed and asked, "Dad, Is something wrong with him?"

I had to explain to my daughter, who had never seen or experienced anything like that before, that this was the way some of the older preachers used to preach. This again was a show for the public not praise to God.

Congregations rated preachers on how well they could hoop, not on how well they worshipped God or taught the Bible. My wife and I recently visited her very wise ninety-four-year-old uncle in Alabama, who coined a new word for this type of preaching: "hooperlistic preaching."

We still today put on a lot of show for the public in our worship service. We have just gotten a little more sophisticated. Some preachers today will try to use their expository theology by mispronouncing and throwing in a few words of Greek and Hebrew, which is generally taken out of context to impress the crowd.

There is so much false and fake worship practice in some churches today that if it were not so shameful, it would be comical. Some people are made to feel that if they don't go along with the crowd, they are not being spiritual. This is one of the basic ways cults influence and take control. The speaker will, say, high-five three people and say whatever. People feel they must respond or be seen as nonspiritual. Some people appear to be so overcome emotionally that they do things that are totally uncharacteristic for a person that is truly worshipping God.

I had my most embarrassing experience as a college student when I attended a church where people did everything to impress the crowd in the name of worshipping God. One of the local pastor's daughters had invited me to attend church with her. Her father was the pastor of the church. My friend, the pastor's daughter, sang in the church choir, so the pastor invited me to join his daughter in the choir.

The first embarrassment came when the music started and everyone in the choir went into their James Brown imitations. They were dancing all over the place. I don't believe it was the type of dancing that David did. I could not believe what I was seeing. They were jumping, turning flips, doing the splits and everything one would see at a James Brown concert. Some would get so worked up until they would faint (pass out) and would have to be taken out.

The second came when the pastor announced, "We will now speak in tongues." Almost the entire church started shaking like they were going into convulsions, falling on the floor, raising their hands in the air, and making all kinds of weird noises. I just stood in amazement, disbelief, and embarrassment. The pastor looked at me and said, "When in Rome, act as a Roman." I decided if that was what they did in Rome, I never wanted to go to Rome again.

I could have accepted this as people really being overcome after being filled with the Holy Spirit, but I can't believe the Holy Spirit would come upon a person so quickly just because someone said, "Let's speak in tongues." I can also not accept the Holy Spirit coming upon a person and then the person leaves the church and returns to normal behavior so quickly.

My experience visiting my friends father's church may have been an extreme example of church worship, but I have witnessed other examples where people have no idea they are being inconsiderate in the way they worship. We, church members, witness these inappropriate things, but no one is generally willing to step outside their comfort zone to correct them.

Some people will stand up and remain standing the entire time a special guest is performing in the church. This shows total disrespect, disregard, and lack of consideration for the person behind them because now the person behind them must either stand or be blocked from seeing the performance.

Sometimes the person behind is an elderly person who may have trouble standing, or maybe the person behind does not want to stand, so now the inconsiderate standing person has prevented the person behind from enjoying the service. "For God is not a God of disorder" (1 Cor. 14:33).

People would get very upset if they went to a concert and paid to see an entertainer and just as the entertainer begins to perform, someone in front stands up. But in the church, it is okay to block the view and prevent others from benefitting and enjoying the service just because one is overcome with spiritual emotions.

We need to face the truth and stop making excuses. It is not okay because the person is not being overcome spiritually because God is a God of order. The person could be considered unspiritual because now the standing person has prevented someone from enjoying the service or performance.

Loud modulating music stimulates the emotions, not the intellect. This is why we have so many intellectual illiterate Christians today. They respond more to loud modulating music than to the word. "Let everyone see that you are considerate" (Phil. 4:5–15). A considerate person would never be so overcome that they would stand in church blocking the view of another unless they just had no consideration and disregarded the rights of the other person. The proper and appropriate way to show the performer your approval, encouragement, and that you enjoyed their performance is to stand and applaud at the end of the performance, not during the performance.

Some will even go through the motions of waving their hands as if they are directing the performer. But the most distraction is when the preacher is trying to deliver the message, some will make cat calls and groans as if to cheer the preacher on. It's like being at a sports arena cheering the combatants on. Is this a performance for God, or is this a performance to impress and entertain or be seen by the audience?

I observed a lady that I could almost predict when she was going to become so emotional that she would have to stand and be seen; and that was whenever she had on a new outfit. There was another lady that had this loud, ear-shattering scream almost every Sunday during the church Service. Her screams seemed like a person who was experiencing the most excruciating pain. The Bible speaks clearly about this type of action: "But all things should be done decently and in order" (1 Cor. 14:40).

Most are in church to hear the sermon, not the congregation's cheers of "Go ahead, Preacher," "Amen, Preacher," "Say it again, Preacher." It is sometimes like being at a pep rally rather than being at church. It can sometimes become a real distraction. In many cases, it appears to be a promotion show rather than a true worthy sacred, holy spiritual devotion to the only superstar attraction—God.

I don't believe every person who appears to become overcome with emotion is just playing to the crowd for attention and to be seen because many are sincere and are expressing their internal emotional feelings. Satan and his demons do everything they can to deceive, and most, according to the scripture, will be deceived. They will truly believe they are worshipping God. But God is a God of order; Satan creates the disorder and confusion.

I also believe that many are just playing to the crowd for attention and to be seen. I believe the best way to spot the ones that are playing to the crowd for attention and to be seen is to follow them home and see how they will respond in private all alone with the same music or that same message the preacher expounded on that caused them to put on such an emotional display for the crowd.

Then, there are others that you don't have to wait to follow home. You can observe just how spiritual they are at church. This certain lady came and was seated directly in front of me during a Sunday service. She came in church late, but as soon as she was seated and the music started, she jumped to her feet and began to jump, dance, and booty shake in an appearance of being overcome emotionally. A few minutes later a gentleman came in and needed to get by her to get to his seat. This emotional spiritual lady immediately turned off the spiritual emotions and gave him the most hateful look just because he needed to get by her.

It follows to reason that if the person became so emotional over what was said or the music that was played with crowd around would probably become just as emotional when in private.

Some of these spiritual people who were so emotional in the church with the crowd around must be able to turn it on and off like a faucet, because I have seen some of them leave the church and within minutes, that same spiritual person cusses out a church parking lot attendant because they did not want to follow the instructions of the attendant.

There are many others that are just following what they were taught and learned growing up in church as a child. They are following the ritual worship they observed their parents and others do. I see little children looking at adults in church and following what they see the adults doing.

I grew up in an African American church and was taught a lot of religious rituals. Many of these rituals had absolutely no theological basis, but we were taught it was the proper thing to do in church. My grandmother taught me that it was disrespectful to get up in church during service without sticking up a finger to get the preacher or speaker's attention that you were moving or leaving. I still see some people in mostly African American churches doing this ritualistic practice even today without having any idea what it means.

During slavery time, the slave master would often have one of his slaves to hook up the buggy and drive the slave master and his family to church. Slaves were not allowed to sit in church with good White Christians but would have to wait outside or sit in the loft. During the service, if the slave needed a bathroom call, he must first put up a finger to get the master's attention and permission to go. African Americans! Please stop practicing this slave ritual.

Another common ritual that was taught and common in the African American church was that the pulpit was sacred, and the only persons allowed in the pulpit were ordained ministers. This again was a ritual and not biblical. The Bible clearly states that after Jesus rose, "at that moment the veil in the temple was torn" (Matt. 27:51).

The significance of the torn veil represented Jesus's crucifixion and sacrifice created a new relationship between man and God. The veil represented separation between God and man because of sin. Before the crucifixion of Jesus, only the high priest was permitted behind the veil to make animal sacrifices for man's sins. Jesus's sacrifice was the perfect sacrifice which had torn the veil that had separated man from God and created a new relationship between God and man so that everyone would now have access to God. So, if only the minister is allowed to have access to the altar (pulpit), then Jesus was not the perfect sacrifice, and Jesus died in vain.

So how should a person praise God and worship in church? The Bible gives us many instructions on how we should conduct ourselves and worship in God's house. Paul makes it real clear how one should conduct themselves in the household of God. Holy conduct is appropriate because we represent the Living God. Paul also addressed how we should dress and our attire, especially women (1 Tim. 3:15). If Paul was concerned in his day about how some women dressed in the church, I wonder, what would be Paul's reaction today in your church?

The praise service that raised and temporarily appealed to the spiritual emotions and the preacher's message that tickled the ear have not prepared the church member for the spiritual warfare that all Christians must be prepared to face. That is why that momentary spiritual high had disappeared when the spiritual member came in contact with the situation involving the parking lot attendant.

The Scripture states, "For our struggle is not against flesh and blood, but against the authorities, against the power of this dark world and against the spiritual forces of evil in heavenly realms" (Eph. 6:12). No one can withstand these evil spiritual forces without being spiritually prepared. While waving one's hands, making screaming sounds, high-fiving five people, and standing blocking another member's view during church services may look spiritual and may impress the crowd, it is of little use in spiritual warfare.

The church should be preparing its members for the spiritual warfare that all Christians the Bible say must face. In order to be prepared for the spiritual warfare, the Scripture states that Christians must put on the full armor of God—the belt of Truth, the breastplate of Righteousness, the shoe of the Gospel, the shield of Faith, the helmet of Salvation, and the sword of the Spirit (Eph. 6:10–18).

Far too many churches today spend more time on crowd pleasing, praising the pastor, and entertaining than preparing their members for the spiritual warfare they must face. This is why so many Christians are defeated when confronted with the evils of this dark world, as the Bible refers.

Many churches today also refer to their church as Pastor Bob's church, or they will plaster pictures of the pastor all over the church and church property denoting that pastor shares the spotlight with God. Many pastors act as though the church they pastor belongs to them. Members need to understand and let their pastor know the church is God's church and God alone. If it is God's church, how can, as in many cases, Pastor Bob pass it down to Pastor Bob Jr. like an inheritance?

Today, many church pastors don't wait to pass their church to their children. Some pastors will have their wives as copastors. Members generally tolerate , accept and then celebrate what most false prophets do in their church.

First Timothy 2:12, "A woman should not teach nor exercise authority over a man," creates a real issue for some of these pastors that want to make their wives copastors. Some have tried to deal with this problematic issue by questioning the authorship of the letter from Paul to Timothy. This only creates other problematic issues, because all scripture is supposed to be inspired by God.

Some pastors will try to deal with this problematic issue of whether women should teach and exercise authority over men by going to other verses that appear to contradict Paul's instructions to his young pastor Timothy (1 Tim. 2: 12). Such verses as Acts 18:24–26 state that Aquila and Priscilla taught Apollos, this does appear to create some confusion. "For God is not the author of confusion" (1 Cor. 14:33).

Satan is the author of confusion, and confusion is one of the best weapons Satan's false prophets use to control and keep people confused. Most people don't read the scripture enough to question what they are being taught and controlled by Satan's false prophets, so they fear questioning what they are being taught. Many will just follow these false religious rituals they have been taught and truly believe they are doing what is right in worshiping God.

In many cases people feel embarrassed not to follow along with what they are being told to do. The pastor or church leader will say, "Slap five people and tell them this is a new day" etc. Without even considering what they are doing, they just blindly follow along and in many cases truly believe they are being spiritual. Followers fail to recognize this is the exact way cults take control over people. What does slapping five people and repeating what the speaker said has to do with worshipping God?

Some pastors will invite other pastors to their church to brag to his congregation about how blessed and fortunate they are to have their pastor, the old "you do it for me and I'll do it for you when I come to your church," the old promotional con game. Satan has employed many false prophets that are doing a real job on God's church.

The Scripture warns us about the many false prophets: "Beloved, do not believe every spirit, but test the spirits to see whether they are from God, for many false prophets have gone out into the world" (1 Thess. 5:21). Even Satan disguises himself as an angel of light. So it is no surprise that his servants also disguise themselves as servants of righteousness (2 Cor. 11:14).

One common and traditional practice in many churches is when a person speaks, they will follow what they think is the appropriate line by saying, "Giving honor to God, Pastor Bob and other ministers on the roster." When I hear this, I know this person thinks he is following acceptable tradition, but he is really demonstrating how biblically illiterate he is because no man is worthy to be mentioned in the same breath with God.

Many pastors use the ministry to promote themselves rather than using their position to promote God. The scripture also warns us about false leaders that use the ministry to promote themselves to become rich and famous: "For the time will come when men will not put up with sound doctrine. Instead to suit their own desires, they will gather around them a great number [megachurch] of teachers to say what their itching ears want to hear" (1 Tim. 4:3).

Many pastors love to be loved and admired by the world, but in the scripture Jesus states, "If the world hates you, understand that they hated me first. If you belong to the world, it will love you as its own, but I have chosen you out of the world. That is why the world hates you" (John 15:18).

God made this clear to James, John, and Peter during the transfiguration of Jesus. Jesus had invited James, John, and Peter to accompany him to a high mountain, and there appeared before them with Jesus was Elijah and Moses. Peter said, "Great! Now giving honor to Jesus, Elijah, and Moses" but God responded, "This is my son." In other words, "Peter, this is not about Elijah and Moses, this is about my son."

Church leaders should gently and politely correct speakers when they try to put pastors on the same level as God. But in most cases, pastors and church leaders remain silent because they either don't know any better themselves, they love to accept the false notoriety, or they fear stepping outside their comfort zone to correct the speaker.

The ministry today in many churches would be far from what ministry looked like in Jesus's day or even the early apostles. The early apostles suffered much in the name of ministry and took very little for their service. The apostle Paul was beaten, put in prison, shipwrecked, bitten by a serpent, abandoned, all in the name of ministry.

Jesus as well as most of the apostles owned very little and didn't seek wealth, nor did they try to acquire much in the form of earthly goods. Jesus said, "The birds have nest; the foxes have holes; but the son of man has nowhere to lay his head" (Luke 9:28).

There are many references in the Bible that support pastors and those that work full-time in the ministry should be compensated and honored for their service to the ministry. There are also many warnings about those that are using the ministry to get rich and famous.

There is no scripture that remotely suggests a person should go into the ministry to get rich and famous. There is however one passage in the Bible that seems to imply going into the ministry could make one wealthy. Satan promised Jesus that he would make him rich and famous if Jesus would worship him (Luke 4:1–13). If Satan tried to tempt Jesus, wouldn't it follow that Satan would try to tempt pastors today?

Far too many pastors today expect to be treated like royalty or kings, like Satan promised in his temptation of Jesus, to be rich and have multiple palaces and mansions to lay their heads, some with golden toilets and sixty-plus-million-dollar private jets.

One church I visited had a group of women called Pastor's Matrons. The matron's job and ministry was to serve and meet all the needs of and serve the pastor. Jesus said, "I did not come to be served but to serve" (Matt. 20:28).

Many pastors today have also created and operate a separate and private ministry outside from the church they pastor. Many of these separate ministries appear to be reaching a lot of lost souls and doing a great job, but I just have problems understanding how they can exist and operate without being in conflict with the church they pastor full time and receive full-time pay and benefits with a private ministry.

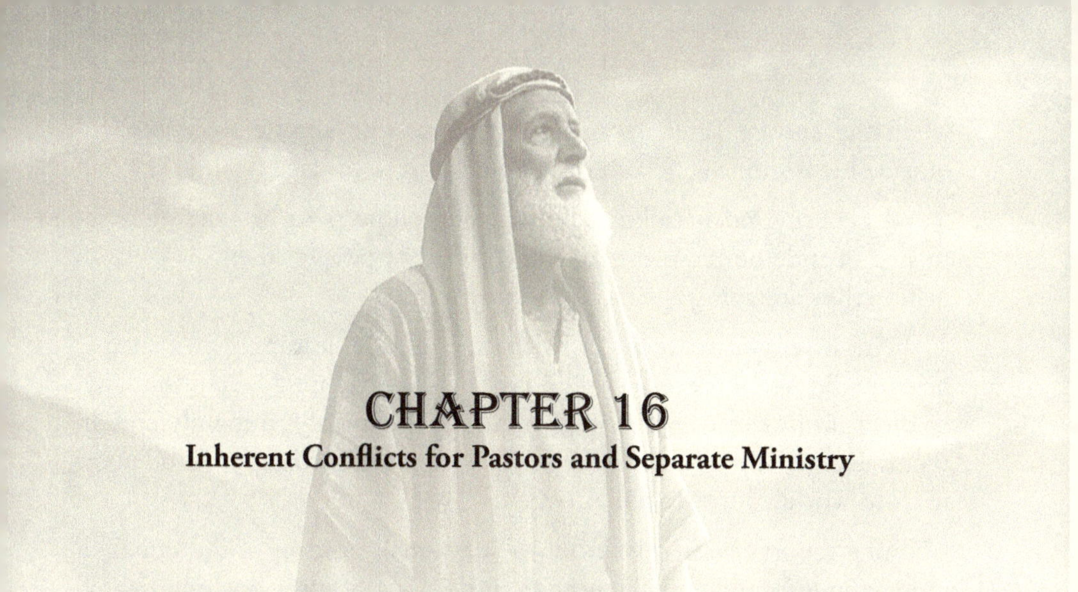

CHAPTER 16

Inherent Conflicts for Pastors and Separate Ministry

One of the most difficult issues to address is the inherent conflicts a pastor puts himself in when he tries to be a full-time pastor and run a private ministry on the side. This is such a delicate issue because it is so widespread that most righteous pastors, church leaders, and members who don't understand or know the scriptures don't care or are afraid to step outside their comfort zone and speak up. While this may not apply to all pastors that are full-time with a private ministry on the side, there are so many that are using the church to aid and enrich their private ministry at the expense of the church.

It is also very difficult to address because many of these pastors are so popular, influential, and powerful that most are afraid to step outside their comfort zone and speak up. Many of these pastors have also done many wonderful and beneficial things for the church and the ministry. I believe God still calls upon us to step outside our comfort zone and speak up.

Saul was a great and popular leader for the nation of Israel, but when Saul began to go against God, someone had to be bold enough to step outside their comfort zone and speak out against Saul (1 Sam. 16:4).

David was also a great and popular leader of Israel. David was also chosen by God and was a man after God's own heart, but when David sinned, someone had to be bold enough to step outside their comfort zone and confront him (2 Sam. 12).

Based on the testimony of the apostle Peter, Jesus said, "I will build my church upon," was one of the greatest preachers of the Bible, but when the apostle Peter became a hypocrite, the apostle Paul stepped outside his comfort zone and confronted him to his face (Gal. 2:11).

I believe God is calling upon all his followers to be bold enough to step outside our comfort zone and confront people when we see and believe they are going against God's teachings.

An investigative reporter with one of the leading news media recently did a report on the millions of dollars that are donated to many of these ministries where pastors are using the money to mainly enrich themselves. Many will claim they are raising money to support the poor in third world countries like Africa.

The report revealed that only a very small portion of the donated money ended up helping the poor, and in many cases not one penny ends up with the impoverished. Some ministers will exploit the public by using the picture of a malnourished child in some remote country in Africa to draw sympathy. It is however ironic that if you google "the richest ministers in the world," just how many of those ministers are in Africa.

Another sinister and con game some pastors use is requesting donation for a prayer request. You send in your prayer request and a donation to the ministry and the ministry will pray over your request. The investigation found thousands of prayer requests—minus the donations of course, which had been removed—in the trash dumpsters behind the church.

There are no two ways about it and no way to get around it. It is an inherent conflict no matter how the pastor tries to manipulate and tries to keep the two separated. It is like a man having a wife and a mistress. There has to be some compromising. Some pastors have tried to justify the conflict by stating they will not accept a salary from the church. That is almost like the married man with the mistress saying "I will not accept sex from my wife."

The secular world workplace in most cases prohibits one from putting himself in a compromising and conflicting position. Shouldn't the religious world have a higher standard? When I was appointed the Dallas County Public Defender, it was made clear I could not have a private law practice on the side because that would be a conflict and would be putting me in a compromising position.

When I became a judge, it was made clear that if I desired to be a full-time judge, I could not have a private practice on the side because that would be a conflict and would be putting me in a compromising position. When I joined a law firm, it was made clear I could not have a private practice on the side because it would be a conflict and would be putting me in a compromising position. I do understand being a pastor is not like being employed in corporate America, but I think the standard for a pastor should be higher than corporate America's standard.

The role of a pastor should be according to 1 Peter 5:2–3: "Shepherd the flock of God that is among you, exercising oversight, not under compulsion, but willingly, as God would have you; not for shameful gain, but eagerly; not domineering over those in your charge, but being examples to the flock." Paul's instruction to Pastor Timothy (1 Tim. 3: 1–7) also emphasized that pastors should not be in the ministry for personal gain.

The Bible makes numerous references comparing pastors to shepherds (1 Peter 5:1–4): "Fellow elders be shepherds of God's flock that is under your care, serving as overseers but because you are willing, as God wants you to be; not greedy for money, but eager to serve." A pastor as shepherd should lead, feed, and guide the people to spiritual growth.

There are many pastors doing a great job leading, feeding, visiting the sick, comforting the bereaved, and guiding the people to spiritual growth and at the same time are still able to manage a private ministry. Some of these private ministries appear to be reaching a lot of misguided souls that would otherwise be lost except for the private ministry.

For those pastors, I have no condemnation. I can only hope they are able to be the shepherd that will always be there for the flock as described in the Twenty-Third Psalm: "The Lord is my shepherd; I shall not want.... Yea, though I walk through the valley of the shadow of death, I will fear no evil: for thou art with me."

The Twenty-Third Psalm of David refers to God as the chief shepherd, but pastors are supposed to be imitators of God (Eph. 5:1) and are shepherds also over their flock. This raises the question, how can the shepherd be with the flock so that they will fear no evil when they must pass through the shadows of death if the shepherd is away trying to take care of another flock (private ministries)? The verse says, "I will fear no evil because thou art with me." God is omnipresent; pastors are not. I leave this question to those pastors to answer.

A friend once complained to me that her pastor spends more time flying around the world taking care of his private ministry than taking care of the flock God has entrusted to him. She said her mother recently passed away, and all she requested and wanted was just a few minutes of her pastor's time during her time of grief.

She said after numerous attempts to make appointments without any success, she became desperate and decided to take matters into her own hands. She said she slipped past security into the pastor's office right after he finished his once-a-week one-hour sermon to see if she could just get a moment of his time.

She stated when she made her way past security to the pastor's office, all she saw was the suit he had preached in thrown across his chair. She said she could see the pastor from the office window climbing into a helicopter like a superstar headed out to the next performance.

My friend's mother, before her death, had been a faithful member of this pastor's church for many years. My friend was not requesting like in the Twenty-Third Psalm, a shepherd to walk beside her in the shadows of death. She was not even asking him to prepare a table for her in the presence of her enemies. All my friend was requesting was just a few minutes of the pastor's time in her time of need. Her pastor, like so many others who are trying to be a pastor and take care and manage a private ministry, didn't have the time just to console her with a few words of comfort.

I realize this pastor does not represent most pastors with a separate and private ministry. There are many pastors that are able to be a good shepherd to their flock and maintain a separate and private ministry without creating a conflict. These pastors should be applauded and supported. It just appears to be a difficult thing to do. A pastor should always try to be above reproach, which means a pastor should avoid conflicts or even the appearance of impropriety (1 Tim. 3:2; Titus 1:6–7).

One final thought. When God returns to rapture his church, will he rapture the church, or will he rapture the pastor's private ministry? Will your pastor be with the church to be raptured, or will he be flying across country to take care of needs of his private ministry?

It has been my intent not to condemn but to educate. Education should always shine light on darkness. Sometimes things that have been done in the darkness when exposed by light appear to be a condemnation. When in the dark people can't see, but once light has appeared, people should no longer walk in the darkness. "You shall know the truth and the truth shall set you free" (John 8:32).

"When I was a child I talked like a child, I thought like a child and I understood as a child but when I became a man, I put away childish things" (1 Cor. 13:11). A child generally follows unquestionably the instructions of an adult. Many of these false prophets want their followers to follow unquestionably and blindly like a child. But an adult that has put away childish things and walks in the light should not follow unquestionably and blindly everything anyone says or does but should test every spirit for truth (1 John 4:1).

The Scripture gives many other examples of why we should always test the spirit for truth and not follow anyone unquestionably or blindly. The scripture warns us that in the last days, there will be many false prophets who will look good, sound good, and who will have many followers (megachurches), but just because they wear the title "minister" does not mean they are not a false prophet. We are commanded to study and test for ourselves.

I am not suggesting or stating that every rich and popular minister with a large following (megachurch) is a false prophet, but the Scripture gives many warnings about them. I listen to popular ministers on television almost every day, and many of them have some very powerful messages. Many people have been saved by listening and following some of these ministers. The Bible warns us about false prophets but also gives us some ways to identify them. The best way I know how to spot a false prophet is to compare his ministry to the ministry of Jesus.

Jesus has given us a model and an example of what a good shepherd should look and act like. The Scripture instructs us to study for ourselves to see if our shepherd looks and acts like the model Jesus gave us. If your shepherd does not imitate Jesus, it should be a message to you not to follow. For the Scripture warns us many times that in the last days there will be many false prophets that will go out into the world that will look good, sound good, and will have a large following (megachurch) and will deceive even the elect (Mark 13:22).

In the introduction, I explained that I believe God has created each one of his children unique, at a special time and for a special purpose. I believe every person should try to understand their purpose for being created and their special talent God has given them and to use that talent to carry out God's plan for their creation.

If God gives us the ability to see things, we know are wrong and we fail to speak out, we are not using the talent God has given us. During my life I have tried to discover my special talent and why I was created at this special time and for what purpose. When I observe and study history and the Bible, it becomes clear to me that someone should be warning America about the dangerous direction America is headed.

It will take someone who is willing to step outside their comfort zone and not be afraid to speak out. I am willing to speak out even though I can only imagine all the criticisms and the attacks one receives when one goes against political correctness, popular opinion, tradition, and the norm.

False messages and messengers should be exposed and attacked. Satan will attack to discredit and destroy. God will attack to correct and convert. It should be easy to determine whether the attacker is from God or from Satan. If the attacker is from Satan, the attacker will try to criticize, discredit, and destroy. If the attacker is from God, the attacker will try to understand, correct, and convert.

Whether I am attacked for my message is not a consideration for me because I truly believe I have been called to step outside my comfort zone to deliver a message to America. America has gone so far from its founding creed and biblical Christian principles that we no longer appear to be a Christian nation. America has allowed so many special interest groups to change our Christian standard to a so-called politically correct standard. We first tolerate their standard; we then accept their standard, and before we knew it, we are now celebrating their standard.

When I was growing up, my mother had some great and very profound words of wisdom she shared with her children. My mother told her children, "The only person that is not criticized or attacked is the person that does nothing." She said, "Beware of most critics and attackers because they are generally the people that stand on the sidelines of life that are too fearful to get on the playing field but can always stand on the sideline where they attack and criticize those that are trying to do something." My mother said these people seldom do anything worthwhile but will always attack and criticize those that do.

I was recently discussing my personal views on the way many churches conduct business today with a very close acquaintance. My close acquaintance rebuked me for my views and stated one should not criticize unless they are perfect. She went on to say that if one is not satisfied with the church they attend, they should just leave. I had to struggle with that for a while because I know that is a popular view. Then I had to come to grips with the fact that most popular views come from Satan.

This person was a close acquaintance and I knew this person was only trying to give me some sound advice, but I also knew this was not biblically sound advice because if only perfect people were allowed to criticize and give advice, only Jesus would qualify.

If only the perfect could criticize and give advice, parents could no longer give advice to their children, because I have never met a perfect parent. The thief on the cross that Jesus praised for criticizing the other thief would be disqualified because he most certainly was not perfect. We would also have to disregard all the advice given in the beautiful and passionate Psalms of David and all the wisdom that Solomon wrote in the book of Ecclesiastes, and the Songs of Solomon would have to be removed because David and Solomon were not perfect.

When the apostle Paul, who also was far from being perfect, visited a church and observed things that he disagreed with, the apostle Paul didn't just leave, as my acquaintance suggested. The apostle Paul criticized and even confronted one of the most powerful ministers of his day, Peter, to his face and condemned him publicly of his hypocrisy (Gal. 2:11–21).

We see things in America today and especially in the church that would have been totally unacceptable just a few years ago, but today because of our new political correctness standard, we accept it. We accept it because we fear the criticism of our acquaintance and what others may think and say. God created a standard, and America and the church have let special interest groups, acquaintances, friends, and even family try to change God's standard.

It has been said, God created Adam and Eve, not Adam and Steve. Political correctness states we must accept Steve as Eve regardless of what God created Steve to be. This is the political correctness standard. This is the work of Satan, and most churches are afraid to speak out against it. I see some of God's most beautiful women today doing everything they can to look like and be a man. I see some of God's most handsome men today doing everything they can to look like and be a woman.

I was so shocked a few days ago when a young beautiful lady I was representing in court who possessed all the features of one of God's most beautiful women told the judge when asked, "Who do you live with?" Her shocking response was "My wife." What has Satan done to this world?

God created man and put him in charge. God then created woman for man and for woman to assist man. God gave instructions to man to be passed down to woman. Satan tried to reverse God's standard and gave instructions to woman to be passed down to man. This change from God's standard caused the downfall of man.

When God appeared, he maintained his standard. Even though woman had been used by Satan to try to reverse God's standard, God still held man responsible and called man, not the woman, to be accountable. God did not create man and woman to be in competition but to work together. Satan tries to disrupt God's standard by creating confusion and competition between man and woman, between parents and children, between the different races.

Satan is still trying to reverse God's standard, and it is so clear in America today. The role of men and women are changing at an alarming pace. In Dallas County, Texas, just a few years ago, most political offices were held by men. In 2018, most of the Dallas County, Texas, elected and appointed governmental positions were dominated by women. The top three law enforcement positions, Dallas County Sheriff, the Dallas Chief of Police and the Dallas County District Attorney were all women.

Today, it is generally no contest when a woman contests a man for a political office. The woman will win hands down, which would be fine if they were winning based on their qualifications, experience, or political views. But in many cases, qualification, experience, and political views have nothing to do with it. It is all based solely on gender, race, political party, and sometimes what labor union the candidate is affiliated with.

It has become so obvious that over the last few years many voters are voting based on gender, race, and party affiliation rather than on experience, qualifications, or political views that some male candidates have joked about changing their male name to a female name just to get elected. I have one female friend candidate that actually filed on the voter's ballot with her nickname because her nickname sounds more female than her real name.

Dallas, Texas, is apparently not the only city this movement is taking place because the United States Congress has sworn in more women in 2019 than ever before and more women have filed to run for president of the United States than ever before in the history of this country, which again is fine unless these women are being elected just because they are women and not because of their qualifications, experience and political views. It appears the God-ordained male leadership role is becoming an endangered species.

God created man and woman to work together in harmony with different roles and not to be in competition. Political correctness and Satan attempt to create a competition between man and woman for the roles God did not create them to compete for. I do believe in the equality for men and women, but I also believe there are God-ordained roles for men as well as for women. The Bible is really clear on this issue.

I do understand why this was such a fertile area for Satan to create such a discord and division between men and women in the political arena. For years, men (White men) had controlled the political arena and in many cases mistreated and abused women. Women were not even allowed to vote in America until 1920. Many African-Americans were not allowed to vote until 1965.

I believe it is mainly because of this mistreatment of political authority by White males that the roosters have come home to (roosters). An African American will generally vote for another African American over an equally or more qualified White candidate. A woman will generally vote for a woman over an equally or more qualified male simply because she is a woman.

I recently had a conversation with a White male friend that had just lost a political bid to a woman who was far less qualified than was my friend. He had to admit that the least likely candidate running for a political position in certain cities today is a White male with a close second being a Black male.

Being a Black male that has lived most of my life being discriminated against because of my race, I can understand why women who have also spent many years being discriminated against will vote for another woman over a man that is in many cases more qualified just because of past discrimination. The problem is, we are playing right into Satan's hand when we do this. The other problem is what would that mother say to her young male child that has played by all the rules; study hard to become the best, but it does not matter because he will be discriminated against because he is a male. Young males are now having to pay for their father's sins.

It is not just in the political arena that roles are being reversed. The role of the woman is being replaced by a man and the role of a man is being replaced by a woman within the same sex marriage. Some parents are even going to the point of raising neutral gender children. Satan is having a field day in America today.

The last place Satan should be having a field day is in the church, but the churches in many cases are now letting political correctness set the standard rather than God. Just as women are taking over the political arena, women are also taking over the church. There are more and more women becoming pastors and copastors of churches than ever before. Is this wrong? What does God's Word say? The church, God's light on the hill, is growing dim when it comes to God's standard.

Many ministers today are fearful of stepping outside their comfort zone to preach certain parts of the Bible that appear to have become unpopular or go against political correctness. It has been some time since I heard any minister preach on the passage from 1 Corinthians 14:33–35, Paul's instructions for the role of women in the church.

The few ministers that are bold enough to preach on this passage will generally tiptoe around the real meaning and try to explain a way and put a different spin on what the apostle Paul meant. Satan has always tried to use God's people to try to change what God's Word clearly says, just as Satan convinced Eve, who later convinced her husband, Adam, that God didn't really mean what God's Word had truly said. Genesis 3:4 is the same way some are trying to change God's Scripture or give a different interpretation of what God really meant.

God needs someone who is willing to step outside their comfort zone and preach the unadulterated gospel and not be concerned about political correctness. God needs someone that is bold enough to step outside their comfort zone and tell America you are headed in the wrong direction. God needs that person who is not concerned with money, popularity, or what the world may think but preach the true Word of God regardless of whom it may offend or who may disagree with him.

The parallels between Sodom and Gomorrah and America today are frightening, and the prophetic signs are all around us. In the days of Sodom and Gomorrah, men were lovers of men, women were lovers of women, and in America today we are being taught that it is not politically correct to say it's wrong.

In Sodom and Gomorrah, babies were murdered and sacrificed; aren't we doing the same thing in America today? In the days of Sodom and Gomorrah, Satan had, like he did with Adam and Eve, influenced women to take on the male leadership roles. Isn't this exactly what is happening in America today? Today in America we are becoming a mirror of Sodom and Gomorrah. How long will it be before God passes judgment on America?

My last request as I step outside my comfort zone for America and especially the church is for us who are called by God's name will humble ourselves and pray and seek God's face; turn from our wicked ways and ask to hear from heaven and ask God to heal our land (2 Chron. 7:14).

The decline of America is more divided today than ever before in our history. We are witnessing a new phenomenon where we are seeing Blacks against Whites, Whites against Blacks, women against men, men against women, mother against daughter, father against son, young against old, Republicans against Democrats, Democrats against Republicans, Liberals against Conservatives, Conservatives against Liberals, just as it is described in the last days.

One of the major problems in the world today that is creating so much division is our unforgiving heart. Satan wants us to remember the past wrongs and hold them against those who wronged us. This will keep us divided. God wants us to forgive those that wronged us, and this will unite us. If we don't forgive those who wronged us, God will not forgive us (Matt. 6:15).

False prophets and people being misled by them should not be a surprise to those that read and understand their Bible, because it was all prophesied and even Jesus explained to his disciples what would happen in the last days before his return. "Many false prophets will arise and deceive" (Matt. 24:24). The Bible gives us many signs to look out for in the last days.

Prophetic Signs Are Appearing Everywhere

The prophetic clock is ticking, and the prophetic signs are appearing everywhere. How long will God allow America, the church, and the church leaders to continue down this road of destruction? No one had any idea of what the writers of the Gospel were talking about when they said, "If those days had not been cut short, no one would survive, but for the sake of the elect those days will be shortened" (Matt. 24:22).

At the time of the writing of the Gospel, man was still going to war with knives, spears, and swords, which were capable of maybe killing one man at a time. He got around on horses and chariots. The writer is writing about nuclear war and nuclear weapons capable of destroying all of mankind. They were writing about nuclear warships and supersonic jets. How could first-century writers know about twentieth-century events?

The fact that there were over two thousand undisputed Old Testament prophecies and over a hundred about Jesus alone that have all been fulfilled should be alarming and concerning even to the unbeliever. According to biblical scholars, the Bible was written by over forty writers on three different continents over a fifteen-hundred-year period with perfect unity.

The birth of Jesus was prophesied with precise details about where, when, and how Jesus would be born. Jesus's appearance in Jerusalem and how he would appear was also prophesied. Jesus's betrayal, crucifixion, and resurrection were prophesied in exact detail.

Most Bible scholars today will agree that more than over one hundred Old Testament prophecies about Jesus that were prophesied hundreds of years before his birth have all been fulfilled in every detail. Each and every one of the prophecies that was made by many different people at different times in different parts of the world were all fulfilled.

The birth of Jesus was prophesied in every detail including Bethlehem being the place of birth over seven hundred years before Jesus's birth took place. No one except someone with a revelation from God would have prophesied Bethlehem being the birthplace of Jesus, because Bethlehem was the least of all the cities in the land of Judah (Micah 5:2).

The exact time Jesus would be born was prophesied: "Therefore the Lord Himself will give you a sign: 'Behold, the virgin shall bear a Son, and shall call His name Immanuel'" (Isa. 7:14). This prophecy was made some seven hundred years before Jesus's birth. Jesus's appearance and how he would appear in Jerusalem was prophesied by Zechariah, who lived in the sixth century before the birth of Jesus (Zech. 9:11–12).

Just how Jesus would be betrayed was prophesied:

> Even my close friend whom I trusted, he who shared my bread, has lifted up his heel against me. (Ps. 41:9, Old Testament)

> Then Judas Iscariot, one of the twelve, went to the chief priest to betray Jesus to them. (Mark 14:10, New Testament)

Jesus's arrest and trials were prophesied:

> He was oppressed and afflicted yet he did not open his mouth; he was led like a lamb to the slaughter, and as a sheep before shearers is silent. (Isa. 53:7, Old Testament)

> But Jesus made no reply, and Pilate was amazed. (Mark 15:5, New Testament)

The crucifixion of Jesus was prophesied:

> I can count all of my bones; people stare and gloat over me. They divide my garments among them and cast lots for my clothing (Ps. 22:17–18, Old Testament)

> When the soldiers crucified Jesus, they took his clothes, dividing them into four shares, one for each of them. (John 19:23, New Testament)

These are just a few of the many prophecies that were prophesied in the Old Testament by many different writers in many different places at many different times well before they happened that were all fulfilled in the New Testament.

Prophecies are still being fulfilled even today. One of the most alarming Bible prophecies was the prophecy that Israel, a country that had been dispersed all over the world, would on May 14, 1948, become an independent nation again. Israel had been destroyed and the people displaced all over the world, but just as the Bible had predicted, the nation was reunited as has never happened and probably will never happen again (Ezek. 37:1–14).

On December 6, 2017, President Donald Trump announced the United States' recognition of Jerusalem as the capital of Israel. President Trump's decision to recognize Jerusalem as Israel's capital was rejected by a majority of the world leaders, but President Trump took the position to step outside his comfort zone to help fulfill Bible prophecy.

Today there are over 15,000 nuclear weapons around the world with the ability to destroy all of mankind ten times over, which was prophesied before nuclear weapons were even thought of. Man has, with his supersonic jets and nuclear warships, the ability to strike almost any part of the world in a matter of minutes. Man now has the capability of fulfilling the prophecy of destroying all of mankind, and unless God cuts mankind's time short, this will happen (Matt. 24:22).

But how could a first-century writer know anything about nuclear weapons? Nuclear warships or supersonic jets? There is no way unless it was revealed to him by God. Nuclear weapons wouldn't be invented until over two thousand years later. Man first introduced nuclear weapons in 1945. Prior to the introduction of nuclear weapons in 1945, the most people ever killed in a war was between 1914 and 1918 during World War I when 8.2 million people were killed.

In 1945 with the introduction of nuclear weapons, 52 million people were killed during World War II. Today, man is becoming more and more capable of carrying out what the first-century writers probably thought was incomprehensible when they wrote that man would kill one-third (2.5 billion) of mankind in the Great War (Rev. 9:15).

There was no way this could have been accomplished with the primitive weapons known to man at the time of the prophecy. This is just another proof that God would have had to reveal this future event to them.

How could a first-century writer even imagine this or imagine Jesus appearing and all mankind seeing him at the same time? "Then everyone will see the Son of Man coming on the clouds with great power and glory" (Mark 13:26). At the time Mark was writing this Gospel, there were no televisions, no internet, no mass communication systems. This again would take more than two thousand years to be made possible.

So again, this could have only been through the revelation of God. Today through technology and mass communication, it is possible for the whole world to view an event simultaneously. Not long ago, the whole world was able to view the Super Bowl simultaneously. Over two thousand years ago when Mark and the other Gospel writers wrote the Gospels, this would have been unimaginable to have been possible.

Another true prophet sign that we are living in the last days is the way people are all in such a hurry. Our freeways and highways have become the danger zone because people are in such a hurry to get nowhere. We are living in a microwave fast-food society where we no longer have any time to wait.

The book of Revelation tells us, "Therefore rejoice, you heavens and you who dwell in them! But woe to the earth and the sea, because the devil has gone down to you! He is filled with fury because he knows that his time is short" (Rev. 12:12).

This is my appeal to America and the church, that we open our eyes, to stop following blindly, observe the truth and see all the prophetic signs that are appearing all around us, realizing and knowing how all Old Testament prophecies were fulfilled just as they were predicted, and realize we are truly in the last days.

Amen!

Conclusion

I truly believe we were all created on purpose for a purpose just as Dr. Mercer stated and called by God to fulfill that special and unique purpose for which we were created to do. Many never fulfill their purpose and their call from God because they don't understand their call and have not learned how to communicate with God, or they are afraid to step outside their comfort zone and answer their call. Others are misled and confused by the many false prophets that have entered the world for that purpose.

I believe just as God has called everyone for a special purpose, God has called me to step outside my comfort zone for a special purpose and to tell the world about the Hays family and how God has been faithful and has blessed our family over the years. If I had not written this information, most of the history of the Hays family would have faded away with time. I knew very little about my great-grandfather Washington Hays and all the contributions he made. There was very little about him that was passed down to his heirs.

I knew just a little bit about my grandfather Walter Hays, who died when I was very young. No one wrote about them or kept any records about their lives. I did not want my children and grandchildren growing up like I did not knowing their family history. I certainly did not want my children growing up not knowing anything about their grandfather Steadman Hays and all the sacrifices and things he did to make life better for them and others.

I believe it is very important to know and understand your past. Knowing and understanding your past can help you understand why you feel and act a certain way. I now understand why I feel so strongly about injustice. It is because of all the injustice my family had to face. I believe psychiatrists and counselors should always begin their sessions with their clients by getting to know and understanding their client's past.

After I studied my family's past, I developed a greater appreciation for my grandparents, parents, uncles, and aunts. For years, I had criticized and condemned them for some of their negative ways and behaviors. I now understand they were only responding in many cases to what they had been exposed to growing up. Knowing and understanding our past is very important.

My dad didn't live long enough to meet or know anything about most of his grandchildren, and they know very little about him. I am mainly writing this book so that the works of my father, in particular, and others will be made known and available for his heirs and others. My children, grandchildren, nieces ,nephew, and others will have available this information about their ancestors.

Another reason for writing about my family is because African Americans often complain that historians don't include the works and contributions of African Americans in history. African Americans need to stop complaining about what others are not doing and do it for themselves.

I began by explaining that God has given each one of his children a special and unique gift to be used for God's glory. Some people will accept their gift and use it. Some will never understand what their gift is. Others will understand their gift but will do like Jonah, try to run from the call of God, because they are afraid to step outside their comfort zone.

We first compared some of the biblical characters God called on to step outside their comfort zone and how they responded to their call. We then examined some of the contemporary people like my dad, Steadman Hays, that stepped outside their comfort zone to answer their godly call and how answering their call inspired others and changed the course of history.

We also tried to respond to some modern-day issues, issues like how we vote or fail to vote, how we conduct ourselves in church, and how we allow false prophets and the One World Order agenda take over our lives and even the way we worship God.

We hope and pray that after reading the life and call of Steadman Hays, my dad, some will be inspired as his life inspired his children and others to understand and recognize the call of God on their lives. We hope and pray we will all realize we have all been created by God for a special and unique purpose to step outside our comfort zone and answer our godly call.

We hope and pray that all will be able to see and understand the prophecies of the Bible and to understand, we are truly today living in those prophecies. The Bible predicted that in the last days many false prophets would go out into the world and that most people would be deceived and follow after them. We hope and pray that people will become aware of these false prophets and expose them for who and what they really are.

Finally, we hope and pray that everyone who reads this book will understand better that we were all created on purpose at a special time and for a special purpose. We were all created with a special talent to perform a special duty. It is important that we understand how to communicate with God in order to understand our purpose and how to use our God-given talent.

I pray the reader will be inspired to want to know more about how to better communicate with God so that they will understand their special and unique purpose for being created by God. We hope and pray this book will inspire everyone to better understand their special and unique call and to have the courage and confidence to step outside their comfort zone on faith and fulfill their call from God.

Amen! Amen!

Don't Let My Crossing
By
Judge Carl Hays

Don't let my crossing cause you pain
For the same God that sends the sunshine sends the rain
When he sends the rain the flowers must grow
And when he calls my name, I must go

Don't let my crossing cause you despair
For he promised we shall meet again in the air up there
So don't spend your time sadly moping around
For I have waiting a glorious robe and a crown
Always remember my crossing is a message from above
It is a message of God's amazing grace and love

Let's just be thankful for the time we had
With such precious memories why be sad?
Don't let my crossing cause you to fear
For he has promised to wipe away every tear
With arms wide open he's called me to be
To a better place he's prepared just for me

Don't let my crossing trouble your heart
I'll be in paradise waiting for you
A place we'll never depart
So, keep the faith for whatever you do
Because God has a mansion, he's prepared just for you

If you just follow these directions on your crossing day
John 14:6 states, "I am the truth and the way."
And we'll wait for you with great anticipation
For on that old cross he made guaranteed reservations

Don't let your heart be filled with sorrow
Because he lives you can face tomorrow
Until we meet on that beautiful shore
Where we'll be together FOREVER MORE

www.ingramcontent.com/pod-product-compliance
Lightning Source LLC
Chambersburg PA
CBHW021623120626
46545CB00001B/368
* 9 7 9 8 8 9 3 9 1 6 3 5 5 *